J. R. R. Tolkien

J. R. R. Tolkien

The Man Who Created
The Lord of the Rings

Michael Coren

B⬛XTREE

First published 2001 by Stoddart Publishing Co. Limited, Toronto, Canada

First published in Great Britain 2001 by Boxtree

This edition published 2002 by Boxtree
an imprint of Pan Macmillan Ltd
Pan Macmillan, 20 New Wharf Road, London N1 9RR
Basingstoke and Oxford
Associated companies throughout the world
www.panmacmillan.com

ISBN 0 7522 6167 3

1 3 5 7 9 8 6 4 2

A CIP catalogue record for this book is available from
the British Library

Printed and bound in Great Britain by
Mackays of Chatham plc, Chatham, Kent

Cover illustration by David Mattingly from *J.R.R. Tolkien: The Man Who Created
The Lord of the Rings* by Michael Coren, published by Scholastic Inc.
Illustration copyright © 2002 by Scholastic Inc. Used by permission.

To David Mainse,
friend and mentor

Contents

Introduction

OLKIEN would have absolutely loved it. Annoying the pompous and arrogant people around him, that is. When it happened, it didn't seem to matter a bit that the author of *The Lord of the Rings* and *The Hobbit* had been dead for more than two decades. He could still provoke an argument. And what an argument it was.

This is what happened. As the twentieth century was coming to a close, a leading newspaper in Britain decided to conduct an extensive survey of which book people considered the finest of the last hundred years. The result was most revealing, and not what some people had expected at all. More than 25,000 men and women were asked for their opinion, and the book that received by far the most support was *The Lord of the Rings*. Objections arose, however. So various newspapers and local and national bookstores in Britain and the United States undertook their own polls. But the results were the same. Tolkien kept winning the race.

The highly esteemed Folio Society in Britain resolved to conduct its own survey, and this time books from any period in history would be included. The Folio Society's 50,000 members were serious readers, connoisseurs of fine literature, and not likely to respond to mere fashion. Their choices? Jane Austen's *Pride and Prejudice* did well, as did Charles Dickens's *David Copperfield*. But coming at the very top once again was good old Tolkien and *The Lord of the Rings*.

Now this did not go down at all well with what is known as the chattering classes — those people who appear on television and radio shows all the time, write book reviews, and generally shape what many people think. First they alleged that the surveys were not accurate, or were even dishonest. Quite a claim. When their accusations were proven false, they became angry and rude. One English novelist, not a fan of Tolkien's in the least, said it showed why teaching people to read was not such a good idea and why all the libraries should be closed down. He was joking, but only just.

Other authors and critics attacked Tolkien himself and made fun of his readers and supporters. It was as though they had been personally slighted, affronted that their particular favorites did not do as well as they thought they would — or should. This is just how elites can behave. Elites are small, influential groups of people who think they know what is best for everybody else. They are usually wrong. What cut into them so deeply and painfully was that Tolkien had always refused to join their sorts of groups. Not only had his book won the day, but so too had the man.

Just to rub salt, and a little ground pepper, into the wounds of the literary snobs, Tolkien made headlines again shortly after the "best book" controversy. In the summer of 2000, as new live-action movies based on *The Lord of the Rings* were being made, the company producing the films decided to release a short trailer on its Web site. On the first day that the brief video clip was available, it

J. R. R. Tolkien — the world's favorite author.

was downloaded more than 1.7 million times. That was twice the number of downloads for the trailer for *Star Wars: Episode I: The Phantom Menace*, which had previously held the record and had been helped enormously by the huge amount of publicity for the movie and by the success of the previous three Star Wars films. Most people didn't even know who was going to appear in the Lord of the Rings movies or when the movies were going to be released.

Tolkien was not only big but he was big business. Protest as they might, his detractors likely would have given anything to be as popular and successful as the man they seemed to so look down upon. As for Tolkien, he genuinely never sought fame or fortune. A good book, a good pipe, and a good conversation were all he needed. He was as at home with the wealthy and well-known as he was with the anonymous and humble.

One can't help thinking that while all this silliness was happening, he was looking down from a place where the books, pipes, and conversation were better than ever, and smiling at all the fuss. A chuckle, a rummaging around in his tobacco pouch, and a sip of that perfect drink they serve up there. And — could it be? — a small sigh of contentment from a certain little character who went by the name of Frodo Baggins. You old rascal, Tolkien, you're at it again.

This, then, is the story of J.R.R. Tolkien, the man who wrote so much, so well, for so many of us. This is the story of his beginnings, his middle, and his end. It is the story of an ordinary man who did extraordinary things. It is a story of mothers and fathers, daughters and sons. A story of God, religion, happiness, suffering, friendship, and genius. Oh, and the story of *The Lord of the Rings*, one of the greatest books ever written.

CHAPTER ONE

Beginnings

HEN we think of South Africa we think of a troubled, divided country. And so it is. But for many years things were much worse as it suffered under a dreadfully unjust system of government known as apartheid. Under this system, black people were denied basic rights and were routinely persecuted, arrested, and even killed. Now that apartheid is over, this beautiful nation is being repaired, but it is taking some time and there is still a long road to travel.

In fact, South Africa has seldom been at ease and at peace, first because of its warring tribes and then because of European invasion. It was certainly not so on January 3, 1892, when John Ronald Reuel Tolkien was born in Bloemfontein in the Orange Free State. The country was divided among several groups of people: black, brown, and white. It was the last, however, who enjoyed most of the power. And it was, of course, into this group that Tolkien was born.

Broadly speaking, two white groups inhabited the country: the British and the Afrikaners. The Afrikaners were usually of Dutch ancestry but also included Germans and French Protestants known as Huguenots. They spoke a form of Dutch, with some words taken from other European languages and from the African dialects around them. The Afrikaners had come to southern Africa as early as the seventeenth century, but the British had conquered the country and the region in the nineteenth century. The two groups lived together uneasily, and would eventually fight a bloody and brutal conflict that came to be known as the Boer War.

It is strange that Tolkien, so very English in his manners, style, and reputation, should have been born so far from England. The reason was that his parents, Arthur Reuel Tolkien and Mabel Suffield, had gone to Africa because of Arthur's work. He was a banker, formerly employed by Lloyds Bank in Birmingham, a large city in the West Midlands in England. The work was rewarding and he was doing well, but to the robust and ambitious Arthur the real opportunities for young men seemed to be in the colonies.

When in 1890 an offer came from the Bank of South Africa, Arthur grabbed hold of it. Before very long he would become manager of a large branch of the Bank of Africa in Bloemfontein, a position of some prestige.

And what of Arthur's wife, Mabel? She was an attractive and intelligent young woman who had met her husband when she was just a teenager. She had accepted his proposal of marriage when she was only eighteen, and Arthur was a mature thirty-three. Because of her youth, however, her family would not let her marry the man until she was older and more mature. She was even forbidden to see him very often. She would simply have to wait. Arthur and Mabel wrote to one another and met occasionally at dinner and dance parties in Birmingham, but nothing more. This was Victorian England. The times were changing in London, perhaps, but in the suburbs and in the Midlands and the north, things were still very prim and proper.

A quick smile between them across a piano, a touch of the hand while listening to a recital or passing one of those delicious cucumber sandwiches that Mabel made so well. For an engaged couple, they were allowed very little engagement. It was an agony for Mabel. She not only loved her fiancé but admired him as well. He was a man of the world, a man of character and toughness. With his thick, drooping moustache that was so popular with young men of the era, with his strong and powerful figure, and with his ability to make Mabel laugh and to dream, Arthur was the very model of the successful young gentleman of Queen Victoria's England and empire.

It was hard enough waiting for the man she loved when he lived just a few miles away. Imagine how painful it became when that same man moved to a different country and continent. Arthur sailed for South Africa alone, determined to make more of himself before he married his young sweetheart. And make something of himself he did. He wrote to Mabel explaining that he now had a house, a good income, and even servants working for him. Would she come to South Africa to be his wife? Of course she would. With her parents' consent now, Mabel Suffield, just turned twenty-one years old, boarded a huge, gray, and rather dirty ship called the *Roslin Castle* in January 1891 and set sail for her new home and her soon-to-be husband.

Imagine the contrast for Mabel between the industrial heartland of Britain and the wide, open lands of South Africa. Instead of factories billowing smoke, there were wildebeest kicking up clouds of dust as they hurtled across the plains. Instead of neat rows of small brick houses and established order, there were strange new buildings emerging all around her and wild-looking men with guns riding through on their horses. Danger, dirt, and difference. She did not like it at all.

Arthur, however, liked it very much indeed. He felt liberated by the country's possibilities. Even his beloved cricket was played in an aggressive style here, a style more suited to his temperament. Whatever she may have thought of South Africa, Mabel was determined to adapt, and she married her love in Cape Town Cathedral on April 16, 1891. After an all too brief honeymoon, the couple boarded a train to take them the 700 long, hot, and tiring miles back to their home in Bloemfontein.

Bloemfontein has never been a dominant city in South Africa, not like Johannesburg or Cape Town. In the 1890s it was even less a major urban center. The small group of English-speaking people who lived there came together for mutual support and to remind one another of the old country. These were good and kind people, but to Mabel they were still very different from her friends and family back home. She never once thought of South Africa as her country, but only as a place to live during this stage of married life. She wanted to go home.

The best times were those alone with Arthur. When he took her hand and led her on their long walks in the country, when he sang to her by the piano, it did not matter where they were. They were truly in love. And as if it were some beautiful seal on their romance, a child was soon born. This child was John Ronald Reuel Tolkien, the hero of our tale.

The name John came from Tolkien's grandfather; Reuel was the middle name of his father, Arthur; but where Ronald came from, we don't know. Ironically it was Ronald by which he was known to his family and friends when he was growing up, although by the time he was an adult, those close to him called him Tolkien or Tollers. He was, said Mabel, such a lovely baby.

Lovely, just as all babies are — but his life as a baby and child was unlike that of most. There was the time a monkey climbed over the garden wall, grabbed some of his clothes hanging from the clothes-line, and destroyed them. Or when he was older, he had an encounter with what he thought was a harmless spider. It bit him. But it turned out to be a poisonous tarantula. If it hadn't been for a quick-witted servant who sucked the poison out of the wound, neither Tolkien nor *The Lord of the Rings* would have grown to maturity! Spiders were to feature in Tolkien's books, and it is not surprising why. The town also saw bands of native hunters running through, armed to the teeth for a chase; wild and dangerous animals would have to be shot by local men to prevent them from dragging people off.

But life was generally good for the boy and his family. The sun shone, there was good food on the table, and Arthur was doing well at his job. So well that the Tolkiens planned for another child. In February 1894 Hilary Arthur Reuel was born. Hilary appeared to thrive in Africa, growing more quickly than his elder brother and seemingly more comfortable with the heat and the wildness. Tolkien had been healthy at first, but as he began to toddle about he started to decline. He was becoming increasingly ill, enough so to worry his parents.

There was nothing else to do but take a trip back to Britain, where there were more family members and greater medical support, and where the weather was more suitable. Although Africa was hot and sunny, it was also dry and harsh and unrelenting. And it could become so hot that those who were ill found it difficult even to breathe. The problem was, however, there was no air travel in those days and a journey from Africa to Europe by ship was long and expensive. Arthur simply couldn't take the time off from work and they certainly didn't have the money for him to do so. Mabel would have to go alone with the two boys.

Imagine a woman in her early twenties with two small children having to make such a long journey with nobody to help her. It is greatly to her credit that she never questioned her decision. Her sons came first. That was the way it had to be, the way it always should be. Arthur would join the family later, when he was more secure in his position. Although today we like to think of the British of that period as keeping a stiff upper lip and steadfastly refusing to show emotion, this was not strictly true. Of course the emotion they showed then was not as obvious, some would say not as artificial, as today. But it was heartfelt and profound. The parting was very difficult for the family.

The three set off on the SS *Guelph* in April 1895 and young Tolkien was never to return to the land of his birth. In his adult years he always said that he wanted to make the trip back, but in reality the country had little meaning for him. He could still recall a word or two of Afrikaans and the occasional image of the veld, or grassland, but otherwise South Africa was a blur seen through the ever thickening lens of a lost childhood.

The three of them were taken in by Mabel's family in King's Heath, which was then a town near Birmingham, in west central England. Here, there was so little space, after having so much — too much — of it in South Africa. They all waited for Tolkien's health to improve, but what was supposed to be a month became two, then three. Arthur wrote regularly but he just couldn't find the time to come out. He was insecure, he said, about his future. There was so much competition from other ambitious young men. All the new men in town seemed to be youths, and he knew he had to watch them. He wasn't getting any younger.

Indeed he wasn't. In November he fell ill with rheumatic fever, a potentially fatal disease. Yet he was a strong man and he fought back, determined to get well and join his family again. He was over the worst of it, he said, but a prolonged winter in Britain was out of the question. As soon as the weather changed he would be with them. The new year, 1896, came and still no Arthur. The truth was, he wrote, he seemed to be losing to the fever again. Mabel wrote to her husband: I'm coming to see you, to look after you. Young Tolkien wrote too, telling his father how much he missed him and how much he had grown.

Arthur Tolkien never saw the letters because they were never sent. Before they could be posted Mabel received a dark telegram of despair. Her husband had suffered a hemorrhage. He had fought hard. Tried his best. Couldn't make it. Arthur, Mabel's hero, lover, and soul mate, was dead. Poor Arthur. Poor Mabel. Poor little boys.

We are tested in adversity, and Mabel Tolkien was now to be tested more than most. In a way, it was a good thing that she had to care for her babies because it prevented her from dwelling on her own pain. She was in a state of shock, as any of us would be. At first the family lived with Mabel's parents, and it was because of this that the boys became more like the Suffield side of their family than the Tolkien side. They did spend time with their paternal grandfather, but he was by then an old and tired man. It is one of the great tragedies of Tolkien's life that by the time he was five years old he had largely forgotten his father and his father's family. Young men forget, and very young men forget almost everything. Dad was a shadow, a slight figure from the past.

Something the boys did learn from Arthur's father and from his sister, their Aunt Grace, was the Tolkien family history. In far off and romantic times in Germany and Austria, they were told, their ancestors had battled the Turks and won great victories. The Tolkiens then had to flee tyranny wherever it arose, and they eventually settled in England. True or not, the stories of their ancestral past inspired the boys. Particularly impressed was the author in the making.

Mabel soon found a home for herself and the boys in Sarehole, a village on the outskirts of the town of Moseley, near Birmingham. The setting was the stuff from which novels could be made. The village and its nearby mill embodied the core of the glorious English countryside. Browns and greens and yellows washing together in a sea of delight. The sun dancing timeless jigs on the cornfields and the ancient barn roofs. Hills and vales, adventure and games. This could have been the land of heroes, rulers, and kings: the Duke of Wellington and Lord Nelson could have walked this road, Alfred the Great and Richard the Lion Heart could have rested by that rock. Everything was possible. It was a lovely place in which to live, and the two boys were very happy.

Then there were the local characters, eccentric but harmless, and all, in one shape or another, would find their way into Tolkien's later writings. At the nearby mill, for instance, the old man with the long, dark beard frightened the lives out of the boys. Worse was his son, who would rush out of the same mill covered in flour, white from head to toe. As he chased the boys away he shouted and screamed. They called him the White Ogre. Another local was called the Black Ogre, after he pursued Tolkien when the little lad had trespassed. What larks they had.

A clash of cultures also confronted the Tolkien boys. They had been raised as middle-class little gentlemen, but they now mixed with Warwickshire farm boys. This was the county of Shakespeare, and many of the words he had used in the late sixteenth century he had taken from the people around him. The Warwickshire dialect was as thick as the cream made from the milk of the local cows.

Sarehole Mill, otherwise known as the great mill in The Hobbit, *where Tolkien found adventure and mischief — and inspiration.*

Because the Tolkiens were not used to the local tongue, they were teased. But they soon caught on, and quickly came to relish the old and steady sounds and rhythms. Cotton balls, for example, were known as gamgee, which itself was short for gamgee-tissue. Why gamgee? A local man named Samson Gamgee had invented them.

The boys were home-schooled, as many children were in those days and as some are today. Their mother taught them languages, writing, math, and art. She also taught them that the best education of all was what they could learn by reading. I can teach you to read, but I can't teach you to want to read, she would say. For Tolkien there was no need for such a lesson. He devoured books like a starving person devours bread.

He read *Alice's Adventures in Wonderland*, the daring stories of pirates and soldiers, and the legends of King Arthur and his Knights of the Round Table. Andrew Lang's *Fairy Books* also hugely influenced the young Tolkien and the man he was to become. One special author to him was George Macdonald, who wrote both children's tales and adult books in a heavy Scottish dialect. Tolkien didn't enjoy all of Macdonald's literature, but some of it he adored. Macdonald was also to shape the author of the Narnia stories, C.S. Lewis, who would become a close friend of Tolkien's later on in life.

It is significant that Macdonald was a devout Christian, and that Lewis was to become a believer as well. Tolkien had been baptized in the Church of England and his family was religious as far as was required by society at the time, but his mother Mabel had been on a search for something deeper than an occasional Christianity. In fact she had been treading a path to Rome, a journey towards the Roman Catholic Church. In June 1900 she joined the church that claimed to be founded on the rock of St. Peter.

Today we think little of religious conversion, and becoming a Catholic usually causes one little harm. In the steadfastly Protestant England of 1900, however, matters were very different. Catholicism was seen as foreign, strange, and even anti-English. Due to the individual Roman Catholic's loyalty to the Pope and because of the political wars between Catholics and Protestants in Britain 200 years earlier, Catholics were generally not trusted and still faced legal and social discrimination.

The Oratory House in Rednal, where Tolkien spent some very happy times.

In both Britain and the United States, riots by anti-Catholic mobs occurred during this period, and in some cities in the United States Roman Catholics were even killed. Why? Hatred and ignorance. The people doing the screaming and hitting usually called themselves Christians, just like their Catholic opponents, but they were of the Protestant variety. Yet genuine Protestant Christians would never have behaved so. Protestants had split from the Roman Catholic Church in the sixteenth century and formed a variety of their own denominations. On the fundamentals of the faith — the virgin birth, the death and resurrection of Christ, the acceptance of Jesus as the Messiah — Catholics and Protestants agreed. But whereas Protestants usually relied on the Bible alone for wisdom, Catholics used the teachings of the pope and church tradition as well as the Bible. There were other differences, but today we can see that the Protestant and Catholic faiths have far more in common than the differences that separate them.

Sadly, this wasn't realized at the time. In fact, Mabel faced immediate consequences. Her own family and Arthur's cut off all financial support to her and condemned her actions in no uncertain terms. This disapproval and withdrawal of support would not, however, drive her from her new faith. She did her best with what she had, and sent Tolkien to the highly regarded King Edward's Grammar School in Birmingham. The school was marvelous but it was too far from Sarehole. The family had to move to Moseley itself, a busy place and very different from the rural splendor they had so recently known and loved.

Indeed, they all hated their new home and ached to move away as soon as possible. Added to this was the fact that the fees at King Edward's were very high, in spite of a generous Tolkien uncle who had resisted his family's pressure and was helping Mabel financially. Suddenly, Mabel Tolkien made a discovery that would change life — and lives. She found the church of the Birmingham Oratory.

The original Oratory was founded in the sixteenth century by an Italian priest named Philip Neri. His idea was for a group of priests to live together in a community, to do good work, and to excel wherever and whenever they could. John Henry Newman, later a cardinal, established the Oratory in Birmingham in 1849. The Oratory was expanding and was a major influence in the city. It was here that Mabel now came. And she came to a man by the name of Father Francis Xavier Morgan.

There are times when true goodness raises its head to the light of history, and such was the case with this forty-three-year-old Roman Catholic priest. He was to become a father figure to the Tolkiens. It is difficult to see how the family would have managed without him. Father Francis was half Welsh and half Anglo-Spanish and had all the passion of his joint ancestry. He told the

The Nave in the Newman Memorial Church, part of the Tolkiens' beloved Birmingham Oratory.

boys stories and took them on trips, gave Mabel emotional support when it was needed, and provided this beleaguered little clan with a link to the Oratorian community.

He also found Tolkien a place at St. Phillip's Grammar School, a Catholic school run by the Oratorians and much cheaper than the grand King Edward's. But Tolkien was not there long because it became clear that he was a particularly bright boy and that St. Phillip's simply couldn't provide the education he deserved and required. In 1903 Tolkien won a scholarship back to King Edward's Grammar School and Father Francis arranged for the family to move to Rednal, near where the Oratory's priests had their country retreat and not too far from the school.

And school was better than ever. This was where Tolkien's favorite teacher, George Brewerton, introduced him to the medieval world and its languages, laws, and letters. Tolkien read the English medieval author Geoffrey Chaucer and his famous book, *The Canterbury Tales*. He studied the Middle English of the medieval era, a language similar to the English we now know but with many different words and a different structure. This was a different world, and one that was exciting and limitless. Finally it all seemed to be going well for the Tolkiens. But they had not counted on the strain that the last few years had put on Mabel. By April 1904 she was in hospital with diabetes, and although she was released to convalesce at home, she seemed incapable of throwing off the heavy blanket of illness and suffering.

She got worse. Tolkien and his brother thought, as all children do, that their mother was immortal. Nothing could happen to her, nothing serious anyway. She was only thirty-four but she had gone through so much. A good, kind, and gentle woman whom life had not treated fairly. On November 14 Father Francis was called to her bedside, as was her sister, May. Breathing was difficult now; the noises coming from her room were strange and frightening. Mother, mother. Be well, mother. Please, wake up. It was not to be. A sudden gesture, and her soul took flight. Mabel Tolkien was dead. No more pain, no more sadness.

The loss of a father was bad enough, but the two boys had been sufficiently young that they had not been too deeply affected. But a mother — when Tolkien himself was only twelve years old and his brother, Hilary, only ten. The boys knew that their mother had given them so much. In fact she had given them everything she could, always putting them first and sacrificing without a second thought. They were confused and frightened.

Yet they still had their faith. Both boys recognized that the

*Father Morgan, who gave endless generosity and love
to the Tolkien family.*

Roman Catholic religion their mother had embraced would now be more important to them than ever before. It had to be, it was her legacy to them. Tolkien was a devout boy who was to become a devout man, and his writing was to be soaked with his beliefs.

Father Francis was also there for the youngsters. Mabel had named him their guardian when she knew she was seriously ill. There was no other and could be no better choice. This bespectacled priest helped the Tolkien boys financially as well as spiritually and did all he could do to be an understanding parent. Try as he might, of course, he could never replace what they had lost. The two youths went to live with an aunt, Beatrice Suffield, on the top floor of her large but unappealing house in Birmingham. It was nothing like home. Nothing like living with their mother.

School helped because school was fun. Tolkien became captain of the rugby team and enjoyed most of the sports at King Edward's. He formed a discussion club with three close friends — Geoffrey Smith, Robert Gilson, and Christopher Wiseman — and was active in the school debating society. He read more Middle English now and had also started to learn Old English, the language of the Anglo-Saxons who had come to England more than a thousand years earlier. Language and linguistics always fascinated him. He began to make up his own elaborate vocabularies and alphabets and to test them on and share them with friends.

Father Francis kept a careful eye on the boys and was pleased with their progress. He knew they weren't particularly happy with their aunt and managed to find yet another place for them in Birmingham, this time with a Mrs. Faulkner, closer to the Oratory where the boys spent so much of their time. They were regulars at mass and often served in the church as altar boys.

The house was actually not very nice; but one of its inhabitants

Exeter College, Oxford. Here Tolkien could study and learn in beautiful surroundings.

was quite the opposite. Living on the first floor was nineteen-year-old Edith Bratt. Edith was an orphan who had been born in Gloucester in 1889 and had lived for most of her life in Handsworth in Birmingham. Her mother had died when Edith was just fourteen, and she had been sent away to boarding school, where she received a first-class musical education. After finishing school, her guardian, the family lawyer Stephen Gateley, had found her housing with a local woman renowned for holding musical evenings. That was Mrs. Faulkner.

Tolkien was just sixteen now but he had seen enough to be mature for his age. And he had seen enough to know a pretty girl when he saw one. Edith and Tolkien seemed to be attracted to each other at first sight. Both had lost their parents at far too young an age; both had managed to emerge from this still able to laugh and enjoy life.

They shared a taste for practical jokes and teasing chosen victims. It was a love made, well, made in Birmingham. But also in heaven.

They hadn't, however, reckoned on Father Francis. He was still in charge and he was probably right in concluding that Tolkien was too young for such a commitment. Wait till you are twenty-one, said the priest, and if your love still blooms you may marry this young woman. This may seem harsh these days, when so many people want all their desires satisfied immediately. But it is a tribute to the affection and respect Tolkien had for Father Francis that he obeyed his guardian. Tolkien and his brother found other lodgings and Edith was removed to the home of family friends in faraway Cheltenham.

This was difficult, very difficult, for both of them. Those they had loved, their parents, had been taken from them earlier, and it was so unfair to be separated again from the one they loved. Edith threw herself into her piano playing and Tolkien began to take his studies more seriously. Always highly intelligent, he had sometimes let fun interfere just a little too much with work. Or, as friends always said, he was reluctant to let work interfere with play. He was expected to go to the great, ancient University of Oxford. But he needed a scholarship because his guardian didn't have the money to pay for his education. On his first attempt he failed. On his second, however, he gained a place at Exeter College, one of the colleges belonging to the university. Tolkien was a man now, and there were stirrings in the distant woods of future story-telling.

CHAPTER TWO

Oxford and Upward

XETER may not have been the grandest or wealthiest of the many colleges at the University of Oxford but it was still quite extraordinary to a man who had spent most of his days in a heavily industrial city like Birmingham. Oxford was the town of dreaming spires; an historic landmark of steeples, churches, and classical buildings surrounded by lush countryside. For 600 years Oxford had played a dominant part, intellectually, artistically, and politically, in the history and evolution of England. It breathed history and learning.

It was also simply very lovely. A walk across a garden, a stroll at night through the backstreets — the footsteps of the great echoed around every corner. Tearooms, inns, eccentric and brilliant professors, bright young people. He could see the deer racing across a park and into the safety of the trees. Or worship in a church founded when the Romans were still busy in Britain. Tolkien adored it. He didn't always work as hard as he could, because Oxford had pleasures that were beyond the strictly academic. He established a circle of friends, played more of his favorite game, rugby, and joined and then also started a discussion club.

Tolkien briefly returned to King Edward's Grammar School to

take part in its Christmas production of *The Rivals*, by the great eighteenth-century English playwright Richard Sheridan. Tolkien played the female role of Mrs. Malaprop, a famous comic character who constantly mixes up her words. According to the other actors and the local newspaper critics, he and the play were a great success.

Around this time, he also undertook some basic military training with a reserve army unit, galloping across the fields and sleeping in tents. He enjoyed the horse-riding but not the rest of the rather boring training, and he resigned from the Territorial Army shortly afterwards.

Back at Oxford, his studies began to engage him more. Tolkien fell under the spell of a most remarkable individual called Joseph Wright. Here was a self-made man if ever there was one. Born in Yorkshire, in the north of England, Wright could not even read or write until he was a teenager. He taught himself to read, and then made up for lost time in abundance. Not only did he read everything he could find but he learned other languages so as to read more. Then, in his free time outside of his regular job, he taught other working people in similar circumstances, charging them a small fee for his services. With the money, he bought more books and paid for a journey to Europe, again to study.

By the time Tolkien met him, Wright was professor of comparative philology, which is the scientific, historical, and comparative study of language. Wright wrote books himself, including works on Germanic languages and a massive tome on the various English dialects. This very much matched Tolkien's own interest. Tolkien visited Wright at his home for enormous teas and suppers and was without doubt influenced by this large, bearded man with his strong Yorkshire accent and ability to inspire young men and women to read and learn. If this was what being an Oxford professor was all about, Tolkien was keen to follow in his footsteps.

Tolkien had gone up to Oxford to study "Greats," meaning Latin and Greek languages and literature, but actually was much more fascinated by the North European languages. He even tried to teach himself Finnish, which is renowned by linguists as one of the most difficult languages. He didn't quite master it but he did learn to read some passages of poetry in the original Finnish, a remarkable achievement in itself.

The pull of languages and the mythology surrounding them was great, but the plea of love and marriage was greater. The years had gone by and Tolkien was now about to turn twenty-one, the age at which Father Francis had said he could approach Edith and ask for her hand. He was counting the moments, waiting for the opportunity that had seemed to take such a long time. Then one day the moment came. He was of age. He stayed up in bed right until midnight before his birthday and then immediately wrote to Edith. Will you, his heart pounding with the rhythm of one of his Germanic poems, marry me? No, she wrote back, I can't. I'm sorry, but I'm engaged to marry someone else.

The wait. The dreams. The waking moments made tolerable only by the knowledge that one day the delightful Edith would be his. How could she have done this to him and who was this man who had stolen her away? It was George Field, the brother of one of Edith's former school friends. There was nothing else to do but go to Cheltenham and make his romantic case in person. A nervous train ride, an anxious walk to the door. Was she in? Yes. There she was, more lovely than ever. They walked, spoke, and laughed together. Actually, her commitment to Tolkien never really had been in very much doubt. She had just given in to pressure from her family and George Field and let passing feelings get the better of her. Yes, I will marry you, said Edith, and I don't know how I could have thought of anyone else. Poor George Field and his family were most unhappy. But that was the way it had to be.

Floating along on a cloud of contentment, Tolkien felt powerful and free. University work that had once seemed a chore now seemed a pleasure. At long last he could fulfill his potential. He studied and read, and when he took his next exams the results were first class. Literally first class. He gained an "alpha" in comparative philology, the best grade that could be awarded, and was advised to transfer to the school that taught primarily English, where he could study languages more closely. This he did.

Father Francis was happier now, confident in Tolkien's ability to do well at Oxford and confident in the future of the young man's relationship with Edith. Only one problem remained. Tolkien was a faithful Roman Catholic, but Edith was not Catholic at all. Not only this, she was also an active member of the Church of England, a Protestant church — the country's established church. Unless she became a Catholic, the marriage could not be blessed in a Catholic church. For Tolkien, and for all those closest to him, this would be a disaster. Edith was willing to listen to her loved one's arguments and indeed had felt drawn to Catholicism in the past. She was worried, however, about her relatives. They knew of Tolkien's faith and didn't like it one little bit.

That must not stand in your way, said Tolkien, because persecution is inevitable if you follow the truth. My mother faced it and so did I. Still do. Edith didn't really put up much of a fight. She felt that Tolkien was correct. Yes, she would join the Roman Catholic Church, and she was eventually received on January 8, 1914. And yes, her family did become angry and she was even ordered out of the Cheltenham home of her family friends.

No matter, she would find somewhere else to live before she could be married. She chose Warwick, an old town in the center of England that is home to one of the finest medieval castles in the world. It is about forty miles from Oxford, and only a short distance from Stratford-upon-Avon, the birthplace of William Shakespeare. Edith had her own piano here and she played it extremely well, giving recitals. Interestingly enough, she would keep this same piano all her life and play it until arthritis made it too painful for her fingers. The instrument would in time be passed on to her children.

Tolkien enjoyed Warwick as well. He was never happy with the inroads that industrialization had made in so many regions of England, and Warwick, or at least parts of it, were resisting the pull of the modern better than most areas. He visited Edith whenever he could, but the traveling and the presents for his love were expensive and he had to find ways to earn some money. On one occasion he acted as a guide and escort for two young Mexican boys as they vacationed with their aunt in France. Paris enthralled him, and he applied himself to learning some of the street language and dialect of the local youths. The trip was shattered, however, when the boys' aunt was killed in a road accident. Tolkien was put in charge of the funeral arrangements. This may have had something to do with his coming to dislike France and French culture as he grew older.

Back in England and Oxford he once again got down to some hard work in the fall of 1914. He was more assured now, engaged to be married, experienced in foreign travel, past his first year at university. He considered himself to be a man of the world, albeit a rather small man in a rather small world. He tried his hand at university politics and enjoyed the cut and thrust and the back-room intrigue. He also won a university competition, the Skeat Prize for English, and was given an award of five pounds. He used it, naturally, to buy books. Volumes on and of medieval Welsh and some works by the great Pre-Raphaelite artist and thinker William Morris. The Pre-Raphaelites were a group of nineteenth-century artists who tried to capture the spirit of art that existed before the time of the painter Raphael, who lived between 1483 and 1520. In other words, they were fascinated by the crafts, art, and genius of the Middle Ages, which was exactly the period that so attracted Tolkien.

He was also writing now, playing with ideas, stories, and characters. During one vacation in Nottinghamshire, the land of Robin Hood, he wrote a poem entitled "The Voyage of Eärendel the Evening Star." The poem is important because it marks the beginning of an exploration in Tolkien's mind of mythological writing, an exploration that would come to fruition years later. The poem concerns a star-ship and its voyage through the skies.

It was written at a time when the skies of Europe were about to fill with objects far less beautiful than star-ships. This was 1914, and unfolding with an invincible terror was what has been called the war to end all wars — but in many ways, it was the war to start them. Empires were about to clash, great ruling royal houses about to fall, revolutions about to transform the world. Why did the war start? Theories conflict on this. But most historians today agree that it didn't need to start. All people now know it shouldn't have.

Men of Tolkien's age were volunteering in waves to fight the Germans, Austrians, and their allies in this, the so-called Great War, or what we now know as the First World War. Tolkien appreciated the need for fighting men but he also wanted to complete his degree. He was so close now. He benefited from a program that allowed men at university to train for the army while at the same time completing their college studies. This suited him extremely well and he enjoyed some of the preparation for military service. He continued to write poetry and to study hard though, and in June 1915 he was awarded a first-class honors degree, which was perhaps even more impressive then than it is now. Very few students attain a first-class degree, and those who do are allowed, even encouraged, to continue their studies.

A celebration was held, but it had to be brief. For also in June a telegram arrived calling him to Folkestone, on the south coast of England, so as to be ready to sail for France. For France, meaning for war. Both Tolkien and Edith knew of the ever increasing losses in France and Belgium. The eager young army that had set out at the beginning of the war was now nothing but a tattered remnant. Britain itself gradually filled with wounded and bandaged men, and these were the lucky ones. Some couples would have seen the situation as a reason not to marry, but not this one. Let us marry now, they said to one another, because the waiting would be too hard.

On March 22, 1916, Tolkien and Edith were married at the Catholic Church of St. Mary Immaculate in Warwick. They had tried to arrange for the wedding to take place at Birmingham Oratory with Father Francis, but that had not been possible as the church had been fully booked. They were married on a Wednesday. Both were nervous, both were happy. A short honeymoon in Somerset, in the west of the country, and then a new place to live, in Staffordshire. Then it was goodbye and off to war.

And what a war. Here modern technology met ancient hatreds. Men became animals, but animals with iron and gas and bullets. Originally the war was supposed to have been over by the Christmas of 1914, but in fact millions of men would never see any Christmas again. Trenches tore up the landscape of Europe and men would die by the thousands to capture only yards of ground — ground to be lost back to the enemy the following day.

Gas was used for the first time as a weapon of warfare. Men drowned in their own saliva as their lungs filled and they could not breathe. Others were blinded, walking towards the deadly machine guns and crying for their mothers. The machine gun was used in large numbers for the first time, but confused generals still sent their men over the top of trenches to stop red-hot shells with flesh and bone. Hand-to-hand combat in the trenches became a martial art in itself. Other weapons included bayonets, designed to inflict the worst wounds; knives, for slashing and cutting and gouging; and clubs and hammers, more like medieval implements than weapons of the twentieth century. The battlegrounds were a quagmire of mud and blood and tears and decay. At times, people in England could hear the huge guns in France shelling the enemy, all those

They called this the Great War. To Tolkien and his comrades, there was nothing great about it.

miles away across the waters of the English Channel. This was not the glorious, but the grotesque.

Tolkien was commissioned as a second lieutenant in the Lancashire Fusiliers, a dashing young hero in his khaki uniform and symbols of authority. The uniform, just like the notion of a noble war, would soon be muddied and torn. Back at home Edith put a large map of Europe on the wall and tried to keep track of the movements of the armies, and of where her husband was. Actually she didn't really know. Propaganda dominated the newspapers, and secrecy prevented Tolkien from revealing his exact whereabouts.

In some ways it was harder for the wives and mothers than it was for the men at the front. The women waited each day for the dreaded official telegram, telling them of the injury, disappearance, or death of their loved ones. Edith received several of these notices because as Tolkien's wife she was next of kin to brother Hilary, who was serving as a private in the Royal Warwickshire Regiment. He was hit by shrapnel on a number of occasions and his wounds had to be reported to his family. Each time the boy on the bicycle came to her door with a telegram in his hand, Edith died a little herself.

But Tolkien escaped the slaughter. Even though his unit went to the Somme, one of the costliest and ugliest battles of the war, he was not hit. At the end of 1915 he contracted what became known as trench fever, a highly infectious disease transmitted to the soldiers by the lice that so relished the filth in which these men had to live. Too ill to fight, he was sent home. He felt guilty, but he had done his bit. What made it worse for him was that he heard again and again of people he knew, some of them his old friends, who would never come home.

While he was in an army hospital, convalescing from the fever, he wrote poems and stories. In the battlefields, he had seen life underground, an entire system of little holes and huts beneath the mud and soil. If soldiers had lived this way, why not other characters, created perhaps from his imagination? He had also been deeply impressed with the ordinary British soldiers, with their humor, toughness, and ability to tolerate any sort of adversity. It will all turn out all right in the end. This seemed to be the attitude of the dockworker, the miner, the farmer, and the office clerk. Whether from Birmingham, London, Glasgow, or the most ordinary farm, all shared an optimism and a faith in good old common sense. Tolkien always thought that the plain British Tommies, which was the nickname given to the soldiers, were far better men than the officers who commanded them. And in Tolkien's books, it is the ordinary people who do the most extraordinary things.

Edith was allowed to spend time with him, in an effort to help him recover. They walked together, holding hands and talking of better times to come. On occasion she would dance for him, and he would smile so broadly it almost hurt. She sang for him too, and looked so beautiful and ageless as she did. One of her dances in the woods was to inspire a story in Tolkien's *The Silmarillion*, the tale of a mortal man who falls for an immortal elven maid after watching her dance in the forest.

Comfort and joy came for both of them in the tiny shape of the Tolkiens' first child, John Francis Reuel, born on November 16, 1917. The name Francis was, of course, in tribute to Father Francis, who had done so much for Tolkien. Father Francis came to baptize the baby, as proud as he could be of the child of the child he had cared so deeply about for so many years.

With the end of the war in 1918, Tolkien was discharged from the army and he and Edith could again start their life together, one that had not been given any real time to blossom as it should. They moved back to Oxford, which was very much what Tolkien had always wanted. He started work as an assistant lexicographer, a compiler of dictionaries, on what was then the first edition of the *Oxford English Dictionary*, a job certainly to his liking. He spent the entire day working with words: defining them, tracing their origins, giving them meaning and shape and form.

The project had been started in the 1880s, but so vast was its ambition and scope that it was still not completed almost forty years later. Most of the people working on the project could not wait to leave the office at the end of the day, but not Tolkien. The structure of his day suited him very well. Good breakfasts and lunches, a sturdy pipe with a strong tobacco, a fine walk to and from work, and sometimes another stroll after the evening meal. And Edith. Always Edith. They were greatly in love.

He was also writing in his spare time and reading his work to friends and some students at the University of Oxford. Reading aloud, teaching and conveying his ideas to others, this was what Tolkien really wanted to do. Teaching was what he was after. Although the work with the dictionary was interesting, it had no real future. Projects ended and there was no guarantee that another such dictionary of this magnitude would be started. The problem was that at the time few satisfactory teaching posts were available at Oxford. So in 1920, Tolkien applied to the University of Leeds, located in the same county of Yorkshire in the north of England that had been home to his old university professor Joseph Wright. Tolkien went for an interview and did so well that he already knew on his way back to Oxford that he had got the job.

Exciting though it was to have a full-time job as a professor, Tolkien was also sure that Leeds could never be Oxford. The city of

The University of Leeds, where Tolkien enjoyed teaching his students and working on a number of Middle English texts.

Leeds itself was similar to Birmingham: industrial and busy, surrounded by rural beauty but not particularly lovely itself. Still, he would always defend the place and once said that students from Leeds were some of his most faithful readers. At first Tolkien lived there by himself, because just as the university's year was about to begin Edith gave birth to their second child, Michael Hilary Reuel. Soon, though, the four were united, first in a small apartment and then at 11 St. Mark's Terrace, closer to the university. The house and the streets around it are now gone, with no reminder of the years the Tolkiens spent there.

Perhaps that is not such a bad thing. The Tolkien children have written of the chemicals and dirt that filled the air, strong enough to rot through the curtains in six months. Baby Michael would be covered in little spots of dirt if he was left outside in his pram, and his father, Tolkien, found that he had to change his shirt collars three times a day because of the grime. In these times, shirts and collars were separate, with the collar being held on to the shirt with a stud.

At the University of Leeds, Tolkien worked under George Gordon, the chair of the English department and a man Tolkien came to admire. Many of the students were eager to learn but they were not always of the highest intellectual caliber. But Tolkien liked them and did his best to help their studies. Although he was happy he still applied for other positions, both at Liverpool and in the South Africa of his birth. Liverpool turned his application down but South Africa said yes. Edith, however, said no. She could not and would not travel so far and the children were still much too little.

In 1922 a young professor from Canada named E.V. Gordon joined the staff of the English department at Leeds. Gordon had earlier studied at Leeds, and Tolkien had met and liked him when he had briefly taught him. Now the two were working together, to

their great mutual satisfaction. They began to collaborate on two projects. The first was *A Glossary of Middle English*, the second an edition of the Middle English poem *Sir Gawain and the Green Knight*. The dictionary took a great deal of time and research, but this was a passion for the scholars. The grand poem of *Sir Gawain* was just as time consuming, and was not published until 1925.

The men also shared a sense of humor and formed the Viking Club, in part to work on translating nursery rhymes into Anglo-Saxon but also, and perhaps chiefly, for the purpose of communal drinking, singing, and reading some of the great northern stories of adventure and heroism.

Tolkien's health was usually good, and would remain so for most of his life, but in the early summer of 1923 he fell ill with pneumonia. After he recovered he spent some time with his brother, Hilary, who was making his living by cultivating a small orchard and farm in Evesham, a town in Worcestershire in west central England. It was around this time that Tolkien was working well into what he called *The Book of Lost Tales*, but what would eventually be known as *The Silmarillion*. But more on this later.

In 1922 George Gordon, Tolkien's immediate superior, left the University of Leeds for Oxford, and Tolkien was the natural successor. He was made chair of the English department and a full professor at the young age of thirty-two. There was more money now and the family could move into a larger and nicer house. But a professor's salary was never great and there was never an abundance of money.

These were good years, with Tolkien a model father who showed his children love and devotion. He was never afraid of demonstrating his affection in public, kissing his children and telling them how much he loved them. He spent time with both boys, sitting up with them late at night if they were ill or frightened and telling them the most wonderful stories. Sometimes he wrote the stories down. *Roverandom*, for example, was about a little dog sent by a mysterious wizard to the Man in the Moon. The children were enthralled.

A third child, Christopher Reuel, was born in 1924 and gave Tolkien special delight. Children liberated him, provided him with a new vision of the world. The ordinary became the extraordinary through the eyes of a child. It was a view Tolkien relished.

Though the Tolkiens were happy, the pull of Oxford was difficult to resist. The professorship of Anglo-Saxon came free in 1925 and Tolkien applied. It was a tight contest, but he got the post when the vice-chancellor had to cast the deciding vote. The circle was complete. He was headed back to Oxford with an important job, a young family, and generous prospects. That, Tolkien thought, was not bad at all. He was right. But this was only just the beginning.

CHAPTER THREE

Inklings

ACK in Oxford the family moved to Northmoor Road and would stay there for more than twenty years, although at one point they moved just a few yards down the street into a larger house. Tolkien was in many ways a most conservative man, never one to make a change for its own sake. He was also a lucky man, because the pattern of his life was most pleasing. Most of the instructors at Oxford lived in residences at their colleges and many were still single. As a married man Tolkien lived with his wife and family and was often able to be home for lunches and sometimes dinner. Most dinners, however, were taken at the high table at one of the Oxford colleges, where the professors would sit. A grand affair, with Latin prayers at the beginning of the meal, several courses of good if plain English food, and wine from some of the best cellars in England. The professors at Oxford, by the way, were known as dons.

Tolkien enjoyed his food and drink but was always fit and trim. This was partly due to his natural build but also because he did so much cycling. Seated on his bike with its oddly high saddle, he would travel from home to work and back again, and around Oxford to his duties and lectures. He always had with him his ceremonial gown, which symbolized his learning and achievements. Sometimes the voluminous article of clothing would rest in a small basket on the bike, but at other times he would wear it, and it would billow like a ship's sail as the professor gained more and more speed.

He was a good lecturer and was liked by his students. He seemed to genuinely care about the people under his charge, whether they were part of the large class that he spoke to or whether they were individuals who came to his home to discuss their essays or have their work evaluated. Some of the teachers at Oxford were seen as dry and dull, and their lectures were not well attended. This wasn't the case with Tolkien. He was able to convey the excitement of his subject and to bring language and literature to life. He did, however, speak quickly and sometimes in a way that was hard to follow. Part of the problem was that his pipe was seldom far from his lips, and words were lost through the gritted teeth that held the stem to his mouth.

But there was also the sheer energy of the man as he raced to pack as much information as he could into what he said. He prepared his lectures thoroughly, often working into the early hours of the morning, but he also spoke off the cuff, giving opinions and ideas until the lecture time was over. Frequently the hour would come to an end and Tolkien was still speaking. Many in the class would have stayed on to hear more — and miss their next lecture — if it had been possible.

The students especially enjoyed his talks on the famous Old English poem *Beowulf* and the Middle English poem he had earlier worked on, *Sir Gawain and the Green Knight*. They thought that he brought the dead to life, made the old seem new, injected color into what too often appeared gray.

Tolkien read in almost every spare moment, and was careful about

The dining hall at Merton College, Oxford, where Tolkien and his fellow professors (known as dons) would take their meals.

what he read. There was no television, of course, and not very much radio. Movies? Not really for him. He didn't even look at the newspapers very often, believing that the passing fashions of the century were no basis for truth. Literature and history were of far more interest and importance. This is not to say that he hid away from the modern world, just that he thought it could be better comprehended by understanding the past instead of dwelling on some of the more unimportant aspects of the present.

The Tolkiens' home was comfortable rather than picturesque. He and Edith had separate rooms for some of the time because of the long and odd hours he kept, and also because he snored a lot. Books were everywhere. Books lined his study; books made for chairs and tables; books formed archways through which one had to walk. Books, pipes, papers, pens, bottles of ink, and cups of tea not finished and maybe not even started would be scattered throughout the house. Of course, there was the ever present large bowl to hold the ashes from his pipe. And in the kitchen stood a black stove that had to be started each morning and that frequently produced far too much smoke and frightened passersby.

Tolkien's children have written about the boxes of Koh-I-Noor colored pencils and tubes of paints that were always in his study. They recall the colors, such as Burnt Sienna, Crimson Lake, and Gamboge. Language. And words. Always language and words. These were Tolkien's tools. He once said that a word is useful not only for its meaning but also for its sound. And if words contained innate beauty, so did a picture. Tolkien also drew and painted, becoming quite accomplished in his work.

Outside was the garden in which Tolkien liked to read, sleep, and work. And attached to the main garden was a small annex in which Edith kept exotic birds that would make delightful whistles

Merton College Library in Oxford. Tolkien was always very happy at Merton, in many ways his second home.

throughout the day. Tolkien enjoyed gardening; he enjoyed planting and seeing the results of what he had started. He loved the soil and the land, and was angered by how England's countryside was being developed and how rural life was disappearing. When he revisited the fields and farms of his childhood, he was appalled to see they had been replaced by urban sprawl and houses without character and past.

During some of the summer months, Tolkien had more time to play with his children and even go on holiday with the family. There were four children now; a daughter, Priscilla, had been born in 1929. Foreign travel was far less common then than it is today, and the Tolkiens usually took their holidays on the English coast. To tell the truth, in spite of his love for foreign languages, Tolkien was an Englishman through and through and preferred staying in his own country. The family would go to Dorset, in the west of England, or to Lyme Regis or Milford-on-Sea. The beaches were sometimes a little rocky, the water was not always warm, and the sun did not always shine. No matter. There was the smell of the salt water, and the knowledge that this was the very edge of England, the border of what was known and familiar. Show a man an ocean, Tolkien said, and he would surely be inspired.

These seaside towns had character. Small cafés and tearooms, souvenirs and postcards, pieces of rock candy that felt as if they were breaking your teeth when you bit into them. And there were toffee apples and cotton candy, all guaranteed to make your face so sticky that it had to be washed.

In the winter back at home there was that crowning glory of December, the time when magic took shape and mystery lurked around every corner. Christmas. This was a special time for the Tolkien family not just because they were devoted Roman Catholics but also because Tolkien was able to see the world through a child's eyes. He knew what Christmas felt like to a young person because he could feel it too. It meant the birth of Jesus Christ, of course. That was a fact. But it was also the coming into the world of a true light, and therefore the certainty that goodness and happiness were real and could last forever.

The children always wrote to Father Christmas, or Santa Claus, and grew used to receiving a reply. Tolkien would take time and care over writing long and elaborate letters to his children, explaining what Father Christmas was up to and what was about to happen. So intent was he on making these letters seem genuine that he would ask the mail carrier — sometimes offering some money — to deliver them to the Tolkien house as if they were real letters.

Lyme Regis, where Tolkien and his family often went for their vacations.

To make sure that the pleasures of the summer holidays and the magic of Christmas continued throughout the year, Tolkien decided at this time to write a story for the children about snug holes in the ground and small creatures and battles and spells. But more of that later. Right now comes friendship.

C.S. Lewis first noticed Tolkien on May 11, 1926, at a meeting of the English department at the university, where Lewis was a professor. "I had a talk with him afterwards," wrote Lewis in his diary. "He is a smooth, pale, fluent little chap." Not much of a start. Particularly as this marked the beginning of the one of the greatest and most productive literary friendships ever.

Clive Staples Lewis liked to be known simply as Jack. Plain Jack Lewis. One man who knew him — Canadian writer Tom Harpur — said that he looked like a butcher, with his large ruddy face, heavy gestures, and loud voice. But no butcher ever spoke or wrote like he did. This was the author of the Narnia stories, including *The Lion, the Witch and the Wardrobe*; *The Last Battle*; and *The Magician's Nephew*. And the author of *The Screwtape Letters, Mere Christianity*, a remarkable science fiction trilogy, and analyses of sixteenth-century literature and the history of romance in writing. Lewis was a first-class scholar, a wonderful writer, and the greatest popular communicator of the Christian message of the century — and perhaps of all time.

A little before the two men met, Tolkien had formed the Coalbiters, a club for professors at Oxford to discuss what they were reading, writing, and thinking. The name of the society came from the Icelandic term *kolbitar*, to describe people who got so close to the fire during the winter that they could almost bite the coal. The idea was that like-minded men, all interested in the mythology and literature of Scandinavia and northern Europe, could come together to share

*Tolkien's close friend C. S. Lewis, known to his friends as Jack.
The finest Christian author of his time — of most times.*

their interest, and sit by the fire and spend the evening as friends.

Soon people outside this small elite of experts wanted to join, and one of them was Jack Lewis. Not that he was ignorant of northern legends, having at one time in his life been a follower of them and having looked north for inspiration and even faith. But the blond gods were too meager for a man of Lewis's wit and knowledge. He was to become a Christian. In his writings he described himself as the most reluctant convert in the world, but nevertheless he embraced the Christian faith with an incredible strength and wisdom.

Unlike Tolkien, Lewis was an Anglican, a member of the Church of England. He believed in some Catholic doctrines but never switched over to the Roman Catholic Church. Having been raised in Northern Ireland as a Protestant, although not a very observant one, he may well have retained some prejudices against Catholicism. Northern Ireland, then and now, sadly, has been divided between the two groups, even to the point of bloodshed. Indeed, Tolkien would later complain: If I tell Lewis of a persecuted Protestant, he will give all the help in the world. If I mention a murdered Catholic priest, he will barely believe me.

Lewis was a bachelor most of his life, living with his brother Warnie, who was also an author. In fact, the world of the typical Oxford professor at the time was dominated by males, so much so that Tolkien's wife, Edith, sometimes had a hard time of it. Nor was Edith ever really comfortable with the round of social gatherings that professors and their families had to attend in order to be successful within the academic circle at Oxford. But she did like Jack Lewis. He was often invited to the Tolkiens' home, and the relationship between Lewis and Tolkien developed. The bond also flourished amidst the camaraderie of the university, amidst the beer and tobacco, and amidst the loud laughter and elaborate jokes. The two men were also surrounded by the other members of the Coalbiters, the group that eventually became known as The Inklings.

People have been baffled by the group's name for years, and even some of the members were never quite sure why it was called what it was. Tolkien said it was a pun, describing people with vague or half-formed ideas who also work in ink. The group met from the mid-1930s right up until the end of the 1940s, usually in Lewis's rooms at Magdalen College. Generally between ten and fifteen men attended, including Nevill Coghill, Hugo Dyson, Lord David Cecil, Colin Hardie, and later Charles Williams. Tolkien, Lewis, and Warnie were regulars. The meetings often lasted till well into the night and much sherry, port, and beer was consumed. Someone would read a work in progress and those present would then give their comments, often not sparing the feelings of the poor soul who had just read out something he had been working on for months.

Hugo Dyson was a teacher at the University of Reading and a tutor at Merton College, Oxford. A tutor is a university teacher who advises students assigned to him or her and supervises their studies. He was one of the people instrumental in Lewis's conversion to a genuine Christianity. Nevill Coghill was a writer and critic who would become Merton Professor of English in 1957. Lord David Cecil was a less frequent visitor to Inklings meetings than some of the others, his work as a fellow at Wadham College and New College at Oxford keeping him extremely busy. A fellow is a senior member of a college. Colin Hardie was at one time director of the British School in Rome and was also a tutor at Magdalen College. Charles Williams joined the group at a later stage, and was a gifted novelist whose books, such as *All Hallows' Eve* and *The Place of the Lion*, remain much underestimated classics. Tolkien was often one of the men who underestimated them.

Hugo Dyson, a fellow Inkling, a fellow teacher at Merton, Oxford, and a friend of Tolkien's.

Tolkien could be extremely critical of his friends' work. It was his job to be so. He had great reservations about Lewis's *The Lion, the Witch and the Wardrobe*, especially the scene where Father Christmas enters the story with special gifts for the children. He said that you can't mix myths and legends in such a manner. To create an imaginary land where humans do not usually dwell and then to introduce a human creation just won't do. It did do for Lewis, and for generations of his readers since then.

Some of the Inklings also met on Tuesday mornings at an Oxford pub called The Eagle and Child, but known to regulars as The Bird and Baby. These meetings were less formal than those at the university and Tolkien enjoyed them. He read his works in progress, a little nervous perhaps but anxious to hear what his friends had to say about

Colin Hardie, who gave the speech when Tolkien was made a Doctor of Letters at Oxford. He too was a linguist and an Inkling.

what he had written. He valued their views and knew that they were honest. Just as a little creature called a hobbit was about to emerge from his hole, Tolkien's stories began to come out from their hiding place. Because it was at these meetings of the Inklings that Tolkien tested his ideas and sharpened his story-telling skills.

Lewis's brother Warnie remembered it thus in his diaries: "When half a dozen or so had arrived, tea would be produced, and then when the pipes were well alight Jack would say, 'Well, has nobody got anything to read to us?' Out would come a manuscript, and we would settle down to sit in judgement upon it."

Unlike the unmarried members of the group, Tolkien could never spend as much time with the other members and friends because of his family commitments. And when Lewis eventually got married to Joy Davidman, a Jewish American who had converted to Christianity, he also spent less time with his crowd of friends. Less time with Tolkien as well. Tolkien and Edith never quite understood Joy, whose manner was decidedly different from what the English middle classes of the era were used to. But Tolkien and Lewis remained true friends. They took long walks together and had deep discussions about matters philosophical as well as personal. They revised the entire English curriculum at Oxford together, putting greater emphasis on the study of Old and Middle English and making it much more interesting for the students.

Lewis and his brother fondly remembered Tolkien spread out in the old leather armchair in Lewis's Oxford study, Tolkien's head thrown back as he listened to Lewis. Then he would suddenly jerk forward and his small frame would burst into life as he made his point or objected to something Lewis had said, perhaps about a Roman Catholic belief. Then the friends would laugh. Lewis would offer him some more of his tobacco but Tolkien usually preferred his

*The Eagle and Child pub in Oxford, known by Tolkien and
the Inklings as The Bird and Baby.*

own. Tolkien would sometimes tell Lewis to clear the room up a little. You can't keep rubbing ash into the carpet and throwing crumpled-up papers into the corner, protested Tolkien. Lewis ignored him and asked if a trip to The Bird and Baby, or perhaps another pub, the Eastgate, was in order. It usually was.

With the publication of *The Hobbit*, which we shall deal with in the next chapter, Lewis was not only loyal but genuinely impressed. He wrote in *The Times* newspaper in London, "It must be understood that this is a children's book only in the sense that the first of many readings can be undertaken in the nursery. *Alice* is read gravely by children and with laughter by grown-ups; *The Hobbit*, on the other hand, will be funniest to its youngest readers, and only years later, at a tenth or a twentieth reading, will they begin to realize what deft scholarship and profound reflection have gone to make everything in it so ripe, so friendly, and in its own way so true. Prediction is dangerous: but *The Hobbit* may well prove a classic."

Lewis was right, of course. But if the book, and others by Tolkien, was to become a classic, so too was the friendship between these men. And when Lewis eventually died in 1963 — the same day as President Kennedy — Tolkien was distraught. He was a friend in need and a friend indeed, Tolkien said of plain Jack Lewis. I shall miss him very much and I shall never forget him.

Tolkien was a good friend to Lewis, and to others, in that he was good at being a friend. For him genuine friendship meant being available whenever a friend was necessary. Perhaps one of the Inklings would knock on the door before breakfast and explain that a mutual companion was in some sort of trouble. Tolkien would quickly put on his usual tweed jacket and flannel trousers; fill his pockets with his pipe, tobacco, and money; and rush out the door. He did no more for others than he expected others to do for him. A mutual understanding, that was how he always explained it.

Some of Tolkien's students became friends in later life, a tribute to his skill as a teacher as well as to his warmth as a person. One was Meredith Thompson, known to the family as Merry Tom. He had come from Canada, from the University of Winnipeg in Manitoba, in the 1930s to study at Oxford, and would become a highly regarded professor in North America.

Simonne d'Ardenne was another student from the 1930s, who was to become a professor in her native Belgium. She and Tolkien maintained their friendship through letters and he was given a unique glimpse of the coming terror of war and chaos by this highly intelligent and sensitive woman. We can see from letters by Tolkien that he knew just how evil Adolf Hitler and Nazism were even before the dictator was universally loathed. Eventually the Germans would occupy d'Ardenne's village and she and other locals helped allied fighter pilots escape back to Britain and fly again. Tolkien visited her after the war and always had a special affection for Belgium. It was, he said, the right size for a country; nations are always in danger of becoming too large, he said.

Elaine Griffiths was yet another former student who became a family friend. She would take the Tolkien children out for little treats and became a trusted confidante of Edith and of Tolkien. But her most important contribution to the Tolkien story lies elsewhere. For Griffiths lent the manuscript to Susan Dagnell, who worked for a publishing company in London named George Allen and Unwin. And so it was that the book that Tolkien had been working on for some time came to its attention. The publishers were impressed. So too would be the entire reading world. The book was called *The Hobbit*.

CHAPTER FOUR

A Hole in the Ground

TRANGELY enough, even Tolkien himself could not remember exactly when he began to write *The Hobbit*. He knew that it was after 1930 and before 1935 but otherwise he was vague and unsure. "On a blank leaf I scrawled 'In a hole in the ground there lived a hobbit'. I did not and do not know why. I did nothing about it, for a long time, and for some years I got no further than the production of Thor's Map. But it became *The Hobbit* in the early nineteen-thirties." Most likely, Tolkien had been writing the book for much of his life. A few notes here, an observation there, a story to the children at bedtime, and a thought rushing through his head as he cycled to the university. Could this ever be a full story to be published as a book? And would people actually want to read it? Surely not.

For those who haven't read it — and what fun and excitement awaits you — the story goes like this. Bilbo Baggins is a hobbit who likes nothing more than to stay at home, safe and warm. He has no ambitions, no lust for glory or adventure. He's just an ordinary hobbit. Which is what? Well, a hobbit is a small creature, between two and four feet tall, with hairy feet.

Puffing away on his pipe one day, Bilbo is interrupted by an old man in strange clothes. This is Gandalf, a good wizard in disguise. Gandalf wants Bilbo to go on an adventure, but Bilbo, though tempted, would rather not. He asks the wizard to come back the following day and have some tea. Actually he is just trying to put him off.

The next day there is indeed a ring at the front-door bell, but instead of Gandalf there are dwarves — lots of them. They make themselves at home and then ask for food and drink and are in such numbers and are so demanding that poor Bilbo doesn't know quite what to do. Then Gandalf arrives. It has all been his doing. He had marked Bilbo's door with a sign advertising the hobbit's services as a burglar (which, of course, Bilbo isn't!), and the dwarves are in dire need of such an individual because they intend to take back treasure that has been stolen from them and is being kept by the evil dragon Smaug.

Dwarves are chunky and well set — much sturdier than hobbits — and Bilbo is a little afraid. Yet when they begin to sing songs of the mountains, of their history, and of gold, Bilbo feels restless. It all sounds so thrilling. Still, he thinks, let them have their adventure, it is not for him. And Bilbo falls asleep. But when he wakes up the next morning, he realizes that the dwarves expect him to join them and are waiting for him at the Green Dragon Inn. No choice now, the little fellow has to go.

Thirteen dwarves, Bilbo, and Gandalf make their way towards the distant Lonely Mountain — where the dreaded Smaug lives — facing danger all the while. At one point they are almost eaten by trolls, only to be saved by the sun's morning light. Trolls are beings of the dark and the night, and the dawn turns them into stone. Aid next comes from some elves and Elrond, the keeper of a welcoming place of shelter in the valley of Rivendell.

More danger awaits. Goblins, also known as orcs, attack them and would have killed them if it had not been for the wizard Gandalf's powerful magic. While escaping from these dreadful customers, Bilbo accidentally comes across a special ring kept by a horrible, slimy creature called Gollum. Gollum tries to kill Bilbo in an attempt to get the ring back, but Bilbo discovers that by putting on the ring he becomes invisible. This ring would feature in another of Tolkien's books, of course.

More scares are to follow. As they continue towards Lonely Mountain, the travelers are attacked by the wild Wargs, evil wolves that are allies of the orcs. Bilbo and his friends fight bravely but are forced to retreat high into the trees. They are saved by eagles, which lift them up and fly them to safety. They later pass through dark forests and are then attacked again, this time by giant spiders. (Remember the tiny Tolkien being bitten in South Africa?) Bilbo fights bravely and as the journey progresses proves that he has grown in courage and maturity. The dwarves' respect for him increases, which was Gandalf's intention from the very beginning when he set Bilbo off on this adventure.

More battles with a dragon, more captures and escapes. How about this? As the dragon Smaug flies through the sky spitting fire, an expert archer shoots him down. The archer has managed to hit him in his one vulnerable spot, revealed to the bowman by a wise old bird. Then Bilbo shows his strong character again, by trying to bring peace to the two groups of good creatures that are beginning to fall out and threaten war. The two sides eventually combine their strengths against a huge dark army of wicked bats, orcs, and other assembled nasties. The treasure is reclaimed and Bilbo takes a ponyload of gold and silver as his reward — not as much as he could have had. But he wants to go home now, back to his county, his beloved shire.

Bilbo returns just in time to stop his house and all its contents from being sold. He had been gone so long that everyone thought he was dead! Bilbo settles down, but not to his old life. He is changed, and the other hobbits realize this. Bilbo keeps the ring, writes some poetry, and spends time with friends and family. All is right. But this cannot, surely, be the end of his story?

Indeed it wasn't. But this wasn't a bad start. The book was published on September 21, 1937, and the reviews were generally very good. *The Times* in London said, "All who love that kind of children's book which can be read and re-read by adults should note that a new star has appeared in this constellation. If you like the adventures of Ratty and Mole you will like *The Hobbit* by J.R.R. Tolkien."

The Hobbit, *the book that made Tolkien famous. It was meant to be read by children, but has also delighted adults for generations.*

The highly influential newspaper continued: "The truth is that in this book a number of good things, never before united, have come together: a fund of humour, an understanding of children, and a happy fusion of the scholar's with the poet's grasp of mythology. On the edge of a valley one of Professor Tolkien's characters can pause and say: 'It smells like elves.' It may be years before we produce another author with such a nose for an elf. The professor has an air of inventing nothing. He has studied trolls and dragons at first hand and describes them with the fidelity which is worth oceans of glib 'originality.' The maps (with runes) are excellent, and will be found thoroughly reliable by young travellers in the same region."

Young travelers in the same region. Old travelers in the same region. Oh, what a joy and a privilege to be able to travel here at all, to walk in the company of Bilbo, Gandalf, and the dwarves. To drink with them, to hear their tales and boasts, and even to hide with them, terrified of the dark forces emerging from the bushes beyond. The covers of *The Hobbit* open like the massive, ancient doors of a castle. Within is a world only imagined.

It was strange that it had taken Tolkien so long to finish the book. Even when it was first shown to Stanley Unwin, chairman of the company that published the book, it was not quite completed. Unwin saw the potential, however, or at least his son did. This wise man knew that the best judges of children's literature were children themselves. He gave the manuscript to his ten-year-old son Rayner. Rayner's response was "Bilbo Baggins was a hobbit who lived in his hobbit-hole and never went for adventures, at last Gandalf the wizard and his dwarves perswaded him to go. He had a very exciting time fighting goblins and wargs, at last they got to the lonely mountain; Smaug, the dragon who gawreds it is killed and after a terrific battle with the goblins he returned home — rich! This book, with the help of maps, does not need any illustrations it is good and should appeal to all children between the ages of 5 and 9."

Rayner was paid one shilling for his review, although we don't know what his father said to him about his spelling errors. Or whether his father corrected his statement about only younger children being able to enjoy the book. On the contrary, it was immediately read by teenagers and adults. As for Tolkien, he was surprised by the reviews and the success. It brought him more than a mere shilling. Just as an example, he won a major literary prize for the book in 1938 and was paid the sum of fifty pounds as an award. His children remember him at the breakfast table opening the letter that contained the check and immediately handing it over to Edith to pay the doctor's bills.

Of course there were some people who didn't like *The Hobbit*. One or two reviews were critical, and from the University of Oxford itself came little reaction. Oxford was, and has always been, suspicious of commercial and public success. Tolkien himself had suggested that C.S. Lewis's popularity after the success of the Narnia books might do him some harm. But the first edition of *The Hobbit* was sold out by Christmas. And the publishing company Houghton Mifflin bought the rights to sell the book in the United States, and again it did very well. The reviews in America were good too, and it won the *New York Herald Tribune*'s prize for best children's book.

Success didn't change Tolkien very much, though. The money he earned from his writing was welcome, and the family could now pay some of the bills that had been pressing on them. But he was still a professor and still a husband and father. Edith was concerned that the family might lose their privacy as he grew more and more well known as an author. This was before writers became so highly sought after by fans, however, and although Tolkien began to receive letters from readers, he enjoyed answering them and found some of them enormously inspirational.

The children were growing older and were increasingly aware of what their father did and who he was. How could they not be, since Tolkien would have them type out his words? None of them were skilled typists but they used their two index fingers to do their best. Poor Michael typed parts of *The Hobbit* with just his left hand after he cut his right one on a broken window at school.

With the success of *The Hobbit*, the main question for Tolkien was what to do next. For a writer, a book that fails is often a final book, but a book that is a hit has to be built upon. Readers were asking what Tolkien had in store for them and his publishers were most anxious to see his next work. He sent them some stories for children, including the delightful *Farmer Giles of Ham* and another called *Mr. Bliss*, and also *The Silmarillion*, that wonderful collection of stories and histories that would eventually be edited and completed by Christopher Tolkien after his father's death.

Tolkien had his first proper meeting with his publisher Stanley Unwin, and while the two men respected one another they did not exactly hit it off. Unwin didn't smoke or drink, but Tolkien did. No, said Unwin, he couldn't publish what Tolkien had sent to him. The books had merit but the public wanted more about hobbits. It is greatly to Tolkien's credit that in his letters to Unwin he is almost grateful for the criticism, particularly those comments directed at *The Silmarillion*, a book that was profoundly important to him and that he would continue to work on throughout his lifetime.

In the meantime, there was nothing for Tolkien to do but sit down and start another book about Bilbo. But Bilbo ends his days without further adventure — it says so in *The Hobbit*. Sitting

Tolkien never managed to finish The Silmarillion *but he would have been pleased his son managed to complete the task.*

in his study late at night, which was when he usually did his writing, Tolkien thought of another way of bringing more hobbit stories to life. A huge cup of tea at his side, perhaps a slice of toast with his favorite jam, and one if not two pipes on the desk, he decided he would create a relative of Bilbo's and call him Bingo, after a toy bear belonging to his children. Thank goodness the name Bingo eventually began to annoy Tolkien and he changed it to Frodo.

As the book took on a life of its own, it turned into more of an adult's story than a children's story. He wrote to Unwin to tell him all this. Good, was the reply, but we wish you could write it a little faster.

But Tolkien also had to teach at the university. And son Christopher had developed a dangerous heart condition, which meant that he had to be at home and often in bed. Always the devoted father, Tolkien spent a lot of time with him, reading and holding and caring. The publishers would have to wait. The world would have to wait.

This was the late 1930s and an ominous cloud was hovering over Europe. Adolf Hitler had taken power in Germany in 1933 and as the years unfolded he gobbled up neighboring countries and increased his persecution of Jews, Christians, people with disabilities, and political opponents. Tolkien hated Hitler with a passion that was unusual for this man who was basically gentle and forgiving. He hated him because he loved Germany and what Germany really stood for. That northern spirit that has given the world so much, said Tolkien, has been twisted and torn into another and quite different shape by this stupid and dreadful man.

When the Second World War began, Tolkien was of course too old to fight, but at forty-seven he could still do something for the cause. He became an air-raid warden, patrolling the streets of Oxford to make sure that people had their curtains tightly drawn so as to conceal light and make it more difficult for the Luftwaffe, the German air force, to find a target. As for his children, his oldest son, John, had studied at his father's old college, Exeter, between 1936 and 1939, but was determined to become a Roman Catholic priest. Now twenty-two years old, John was in Rome training in a seminary to become a priest when the city began to fill with German soldiers. He realized that this was no place for a young Englishman and embarked on a five-day journey to Paris, and then made it onto what turned out to be the last boat from the French coast back to Britain. He and his fellow students from the seminary spent the rest of the war in the north of England, and John was eventually ordained as a priest at the beginning of 1946.

His brothers joined the armed forces. Michael, now entering his twenties, was in the army and served defending airfields in Britain and later in France and Germany. Christopher, who had been so ill but was now recovered, trained as a pilot in the Royal Air Force while still in his late teens. Oddly enough he did some of his training in South Africa, the country of his father's birth. Priscilla, who was the youngest child and around ten years old now, stayed at home, giving much needed help to Edith.

Tolkien arranged special lectures for members of the military during this time, but he also continued working on his new hobbit book. Just before the war started, just as the British prime minister Neville Chamberlain signed an agreement with Hitler in a feeble effort to maintain peace, Tolkien thought of a title for his project. It would be called *The Lord of the Rings*.

He worked less on the book during the war years because there was simply so much else to do. The Tolkiens bought some hens in order to help with the food supply. Basic foods were being rationed because of the blockade of Britain by the German navy and because of the need to feed Britain's soldiers and sailors. They took in lodgers and people who had been evacuated from the major cities due to the German bombing raids. Oxford itself was never bombed, as it turned out. Probably not, as Tolkien used to say afterwards, because they knew what a fine warden he was!

Professor Tolkien, 1955.

Other towns were not so lucky. Coventry was almost totally dev-
astated by a huge German attack one night, and that city was only
forty miles from Oxford. It was so close that Tolkien was able to see
the glow of fire as he looked out of his study window. The war
touched everybody. The family worried about their two boys who
were serving, and they themselves had to cope with rationing and
very little food. They grew vegetables in the garden and cut back
wherever they could. It was tough, but they knew it wasn't as tough
as it could be. Their radio told them what was happening in Europe
and Tolkien was in despair at the slaughter and the misery.

The writing helped him. Some would argue later that *The Lord of
the Rings* was influenced by the war and world events, but Tolkien

said no, we must not read too much of all that into his work. Part of the book's glory, however, is that it can be understood and appreciated on so many levels. This was what he told his publishers as he sent them more and more chapters of the new work. He sent parts of it to his son Christopher, as well, with accompanying letters asking for suggestions and ideas. Edith was also an able and enthusiastic critic; Tolkien always told his wife what he was writing and showed her some of his work in progress. Help also came from Jack Lewis, who pushed his friend on when Tolkien found it difficult to return to the book. This was hard work, and turning out to be a much less enjoyable experience than the writing of *The Hobbit*.

In 1945 Tolkien was made Merton Professor of English Language and Literature with special responsibility for Middle English up to 1500, a position that he would hold right up until his retirement in 1959. Merton College owned several properties, both in Oxford and outside the city, and offered one of its Oxford homes to Tolkien. Such was the affection Oxford and its people had for Tolkien. The family resisted the pull away from Northmoor Road but in 1947 they finally moved to Manor Road, into a house that was actually far less roomy than what they were used to. The move also represented an emotional shift because the children had grown used to their old home and the change of house seemed to mean greater changes and a time of growing up.

The war was over and Tolkien's university life returned to normal. It was a different world now, though, and one that was far less innocent than it had been before 1939. *The Hobbit* was reprinted and *Farmer Giles of Ham* was finally accepted for publication. Tolkien was in his fifties now and was slowing down just a little. Gradually the children left home and in turn started their own families. Michael and Christopher gave Tolkien and Edith grandchildren, and their visits were always a source of great entertainment. None of the work and all of the fun of having children, Tolkien would say, smiling at his sons with his broad and friendly grin. As the family changed in size, and as Oxford became busier and louder, the Tolkiens moved again, eventually to nearby Headington, a town of a few thousand people not far from where Jack Lewis lived.

Merton College was more modern in its ways than some of the other Oxford colleges, but there were still fine old characters about. One of the best of them was an old professor by the name of Garrod, who taught classics. He was known throughout Merton, throughout Oxford, for his eccentricities and his wit. He could be seen regularly walking around the town smoking a cigar and accompanied by his little dog. A famous story about him goes that during the First World War a lady saw him reading a book in a city bookstore. She angrily demanded to know why with so many other men in France fighting he was not there with them doing his bit for the defense of civilization. "Madam," he said, barely even lifting his head from his book, "I am civilization."

Tolkien felt comfortable at Merton, especially when his old friends Hugo Dyson and Nevill Coghill were appointed to positions at the college. They could pass time together discussing how Oxford was changing, how everything was changing. Tolkien's rooms at the college dated from the seventeenth century, and from their windows he could gaze out on stretches of green meadow that hadn't changed very much since Merton itself had been built all those hundreds of years ago.

Lewis would visit him often and the two men would talk about some of the mail they had received from enthusiastic readers. Lewis would also insist on asking Tolkien how *The Lord of the Rings* was coming. You have to finish it, he said, for everybody's sake. What a

Merton College Library, where Tolkien spent so many hours of study and writing.

tragedy if it remained half complete and never saw publication. Then, so suddenly that it surprised him, Lewis was told by his friend that the book was finished. Let me read it, Lewis insisted. All right, he could. And he did, and he then wrote to the author.

"I have drained the rich cup and satisfied a long thirst," Lewis said. "Once it really gets under way, the steady upward slope of grandeur and terror (not unrelieved by green dells, without which it would indeed be intolerable) is almost unequalled in the whole range of narrative art known to me. In two virtues I think it excels: sheer sub-creation — Bombadil, Barrow-wights, Elves, Ents — as if from inexhaustible resources, and construction. Also in *gravitas*." This was enough for Tolkien. If Jack Lewis could be so enthusiastic, then the book was ready. Now was the time for the coming of *The Lord of the Rings*.

CHAPTER FIVE

His Lordship of the Rings

ND so it was finished. But what to do now? The book had taken twelve years to write and Tolkien told his friends that this was a product not only of inspiration and imagination but also of blood, sweat, and tears. Edith was a constant companion and help at this time, as she was throughout their marriage. Whenever Tolkien grew tired of his work, his wife would come to his rescue, reminding him how important it was and just how gifted he was as a writer. A smile here and a cup of tea there were of worth beyond compare.

Allen and Unwin was anxious to bring out the book but Tolkien's enthusiasm for the publisher had waned over the years. He had been gracious when it had rejected some of his earlier works, but the more he thought about it the more he felt that a publisher's commitment should be total and not so selective. In the meantime, he had also met Milton Waldman from another publishing house, Collins, and become quite friendly with him. Not only was Waldman a Catholic with views similar to those of Tolkien, but the two men had a mutual friend in Gervase Mathew, a Roman Catholic priest and sometime Inkling. Tolkien showed Waldman *The Silmarillion* and Waldman said that, as long as Tolkien could finish it, Collins would publish this remarkable book.

Waldman was then shown *The Lord of the Rings* and he was equally enthusiastic. Tolkien was delighted. His present publisher had, he thought, not done a very good job with one of the reprints of *The Hobbit*, and had done hardly anything to promote *Farmer Giles of Ham*, a book that was allowed to fade away. There was, however, a problem. Tolkien had signed a contract with Allen and Unwin and he couldn't just walk off to another publisher. He sent Sir Stanley, recently knighted, the manuscript of his new book but added a letter almost inviting him to reject it. Unwin wasn't to be put off so easily. He in turn sent the work to his son Rayner, who as a boy had said so many kind things about *The Hobbit*. Rayner recommended publishing *The Lord of the Rings*, though with some editing, and they both said no once again to *The Silmarillion*. There was more correspondence between Stanley Unwin and Tolkien, but finally Unwin gave up the fight and said that if Tolkien was insisting on the publication of both books then he had to turn him down. Tolkien gave a deep sigh of relief. He was free.

But matters were not as simple as they seemed. William Collins, from the Collins publishing house, wanted some cutting of *The Lord of the Rings*, and Waldman was surprised at the growing length of *The Silmarillion*. Months went by, and then years. By 1952 neither book had been published. It's strange today to think that *The Lord of the Rings*, a book of such massive commercial and literary success, should have remained unpublished for so long. The author eventually wrote again to Allen and Unwin in London, this time to the sympathetic Rayner, who was now working there. Not an easy letter to write, as it meant Tolkien would have to humble himself. But Rayner was not a person to gloat. Of course he would love to have *The Lord of the Rings*, send it at once. Send it? No, said Tolkien. He had only one copy of the manuscript. There were no

The Lord of the Rings, *quite simply one of the most successful books in the history of literature.*

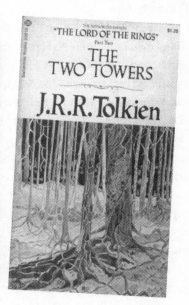

word processors then and, because of the scarcities caused by the war, paper was in short supply and the manuscript was particularly long. Too long, in fact, for him to get a copy made. He would meet with Rayner to hand it over in person.

They met in Oxford in September 1952 and Rayner took the manuscript back to London with him. It was such a large work that he decided it could not be published in one book but should appear in three volumes. Rayner wrote to his father, Sir Stanley, to finalize the arrangements. He explained that because the book was so large and would best be presented as a trilogy, the profit margin would not be great. The company could lose a lot of money if it wasn't a success. But, in his opinion, it was such a remarkable book that they had to proceed. Sir Stanley did not have to consider the proposal for very long. He said yes. It was one of those defining moments in literary history.

There were contracts to be signed and some editing to be done. Tolkien was not going to earn as much money from the work as he had hoped, but if the book sold well over the years he might be all right. The first volume, *The Fellowship of the Ring*, would appear in the summer of 1954 and the other two volumes, *The Two Towers* and *The Return of the King*, would follow soon afterwards. The initial print run of the first volume would be around 3,500 only, since interest would, the publishers thought, not be so great. And then, and then. The story of the trilogy is as follows.

It is sixty years since Bilbo returned from his tremendous adventure. He decides to give a birthday party and during the celebrations announces that he is leaving the Shire to see the places he has only heard and read about. He gives presents out to his old friends and relatives and then, quite suddenly, puts the magic ring on his finger and disappears, later reappearing in his house. Bilbo leaves everything except the ring to his young cousin Frodo, but is persuaded by Gandalf to then include the ring in his legacy. It is significant that Bilbo, completely out of character, becomes violent and aggressive when Gandalf first asks this of him. We'll come back to this later in the story.

The ring is in fact the One Ring of Power, and because of it important things are occurring in the greater world. The good creatures, the Free Folk, are having a tough time against their dark enemies. Gandalf persuades Frodo, along with three other hobbits — Merry, Pippin, and Sam — to leave the Shire with the ring. They are uncertain about going but must do so to save the lives of their friends, who will be in danger if the ring is found. Now the adventures begin again.

The terrifying Black Riders of Mordor nearly capture and kill the little heroes, who are helped and saved by a character called Strider. They reach the valley of Rivendell and the Council of Elrond, where it is decided that the ring must be destroyed. But how to destroy it? The only place where this is possible is the Mountain of Fire in Mordor, and to reach this place entails a long and dangerous journey. Sauron, the Lord of Mordor, is conquering all before him and he wants the ring in order to complete his power and become supreme. Frodo and the three other hobbits set forth, accompanied by a group that includes Gimli the dwarf, Legolas the elf, Strider, who is also known as Aragorn, and Boromir. Boromir is a warrior and human lord of Minas Tirith, one of the strongholds against darkness.

They are led by Gandalf into the Mines of Moria, where the wizard is attacked by an evil spirit, a Balrog, and disappears into what seems to be a bottomless pit. More frights and fears, until the company reaches Lothlórien and is given strength to continue by a beautiful lady of that elvish land who goes by the name of Galadriel. The group splits up at the Falls of Rauros, and Gollum, back again from *The Hobbit*, is now after them and anxious to get his ring back. Merry and Pippin are in one group; Legolas, Gimli, and Aragorn in another; and Sam and Frodo in yet another. The ring's power intervenes again, maddening Boromir just as it had Bilbo near the beginning of this story. Boromir attacks Frodo and almost catches him. But the orcs then attack and Boromir once more becomes himself, fighting skillfully and bravely against the orcs until their numbers overwhelm him and he is killed. His actions, however, have saved the lives of Merry and Pippin.

Next there are encounters with talking trees, more escapes from the orcs, and the discovery of a formerly good wizard who has been seduced by darkness. But still the journey continues. Gandalf enters the story once again, nobler and stronger since his fight with the evil spirit. Riding on a fine horse called Shadowfax, Gandalf leads Aragorn, Gimli, and Legolas to King Théoden's hall in Rohan. An evil adviser named Wormtongue is overcome, and the king is liberated from a spell cast upon him. Forces of good are joined and a great battle is fought at Hornburg, and the armies of light are victorious. It looks as if the great struggle is almost over. Not so. There are still winged creatures called Ringwraiths, castle strongholds, the Pass of the Spider, and the Great War of the Ring.

As the brave little hobbits continue on, the ring becomes heavier and its strange attraction ever stronger. Frodo is wounded in battle and captured by orcs. The tide is turning, but in the wrong direction. Castles are besieged and coalitions of wicked armies arranged, and unless help arrives the world will fall to darkness. Then the forces of Rohan appear and, helped by Aragorn with his seaborne troops, the battle is won. And what is happening with Frodo and Sam? They have finally reached the Mountain of Fire — also known as Mount Doom — where the ring can be destroyed. Yet the ring's power and Frodo's weakness of will after such efforts make it almost impossible for him to part with it. But Gollum, who has been following the pair all this way, makes a desperate leap for the ring and grabs it from Frodo, biting off the young hobbit's finger along with it. Crazed and desperate, Gollum loses balance and plunges into the furnace below, gone forever, along with the ring itself.

As the ring is destroyed, the power of Mordor and darkness is finished. The entire earth shakes at this, dark clouds fill the sky, and Gandalf arrives on an enormous eagle to help Frodo and Sam. The two are treated as heroes. All of them make their way back to the Shire, amidst great celebrations and parties. Yet there is still more to come. Back at the Shire the hobbits find that a band of ruffians under the Boss, their leader, has taken over most of the region. Lotho Simple, an unscrupulous hobbit, had sold off hobbit land for profit and broken up all the fine traditions and families. The hobbits themselves had changed with the times, and the times were dominated by the dirty and rude ruffians.

Frodo and Sam are different now, though, and have seen and done enough to be able to stand up for themselves and for others. After some difficult fights and arguments, they confront the ruffian leader, who turns out to be an evil wizard they had earlier encountered, with Wormtongue behind him. Although Frodo is now too tired to win this one final struggle, the ruffian leaders fall out among themselves and eventually the Shire returns to something like its old glory and happiness.

Frodo becomes somewhat reclusive. His battle wound aches and he has known more than enough adventure. He helps the aged

Bilbo, who appears near the end of the story, record their story for posterity, until one day Frodo calls for Sam and rides off to the Grey Havens. From there, Frodo is joined by a very old Bilbo, and together they sail away to the West. As the ship fades into the rain-filled night, farther and farther, Sam looks on, so sad but so understanding at his friend's departure. Then, just for a moment, the silver-glass curtain of rain rolls back and Sam glimpses a wonderfully green and pleasing land, like something out of a vision. The Fourth Age of Middle-earth begins, and good old Sam returns home. To the Shire.

That, in the briefest of tellings, is the story of *The Lord of the Rings*. Ever since publication, critics and scholars have tried to search for and interpret symbols. All very well, of course, but the book doesn't require any of that at all. Of course there are some obvious influences. Tolkien was a dedicated Roman Catholic and the book is packed with Christian references. But one need not be a Christian to enjoy it. The dark figures no doubt reflect what Tolkien saw as present-day threats: industrialization, the destruction of country life, pollution, the loss of tradition. But, again, one hardly has to think about these issues to be won over by *The Lord of the Rings*.

And won over most people were. The majority of the reviews were extremely good. Good enough, in fact, for the initial printing of 3,500 copies to be sold out in just over a month. Newspapers and magazines in Britain and in the United States — where it was published by Houghton Mifflin in 1955 — were startled by the book's originality and depth. *The Observer* in London said that this was "an extraordinary book. It deals with a stupendous theme. It leads us through a succession of strange and astonishing episodes, some of them magnificent, in a region where everything is invented, forest, moor, river, wilderness, town, and the races which inhabit them." London's *Sunday Telegraph* thought it "among the greatest works of imaginative fiction of the twentieth century" and *The Times* said that "the story moves on with a tremendous narrative rush to its climax" and concluded that it was an "extraordinarily imaginative work, part saga, part allegory, and wholly exciting."

Translations were requested, and over the years the book has appeared in most of the world's languages, including Japanese, Vietnamese, and Hebrew. Concerning the last, some have compared Tolkien's love for all things northern — such as the Norse mythology of the Vikings, and the romantic visions of snow-topped hills and lush green valleys — with the crazed Nazi notion of Aryan superiority. When *The Lord of the Rings* was published, a few viewed it as a critique of the modern world and a longing for the past. In a way it was. But could this be, one critic asked, something to do with fascism — the murderous ideology held by dictators such as Hitler and Mussolini?

The answer is a solid no. Shortly before the Second World War, a German publisher was interested in buying the rights to translate *The Hobbit* into German. The publishing house asked if Tolkien was an Aryan. Tolkien was outraged. He replied that the term meant nothing. If, however, the publisher was in fact asking if he had any Jewish blood, he regretted that this was not the case. He would have liked, he said, to have some connection to such a gifted people, but sadly he did not. He did, however, he added, have close Jewish friends. And, as a final suggestion, would these German people with their insane ideas please go and hang themselves because he wanted absolutely nothing to do with them. This was at a time when some leading politicians and writers were flirting with Nazism.

But the war was over now and Tolkien could enjoy the success that was sweeping over him like some refreshing, warm water wave. As each of the three volumes was published, the readership increased. Letters began to arrive, first a steady trickle, then a steady flow, and finally a steady flood. And they came from all over the world. This was something Tolkien had not reckoned with, and he asked Edith what he should do. Reply to them, of course. Some of Tolkien's colleagues at the university, unfortunately, were disapproving. They preferred the outside world to keep as far away as possible from the halls of academe. Never mind, thought Tolkien, let them have their privacy. I can carry on my personal and professional life and still write books that are read by so many people.

The British Broadcasting Corporation approached Tolkien with the idea of turning *The Lord of the Rings* into a radio play. This might be acceptable. Some American film producers approached him with the idea of turning the book into a movie. But in their proposal they misspelled the names of some of the leading characters. This, he thought, was less acceptable. Still, the excitement was surely a good thing. Problems came up, too, however. One publisher in the United States, Ace Books, thought it could take advantage of the vague copyright laws between Britain and the United States and issue a paperback edition of the book without paying any money to its author. The publisher was right. Its edition was produced cheaply and with some printing errors. Nevertheless, in the single year of 1965, *The Lord of the Rings* sold more than 100,000 copies.

Tolkien's official publisher in the United States, Houghton Mifflin, produced an authorized single-volume paperback edition with Ballantine Books and this also sold very well. American students in particular flocked to the book and its ideas. As has happened

Tolkien, only a few months before his death. Happiness, which is evident by the smile on his face, was a quality he admired and possessed.

HIS LORDSHIP OF THE RINGS

in the past and continues to happen today, British authors have been made truly famous and financially secure by the response of a market 3,000 miles away. The book outsold all others on university and college campuses across North America, including the most elitist of institutions, the Ivy League universities. Students scrawled graffiti on walls and wore badges calling for Frodo to be made president. Tolkien and Hobbit societies began to be formed on three continents, university English departments introduced lectures on *The Lord of the Rings*, television companies visited Tolkien in Oxford to make programs about him, and American academics began to write books about Tolkien and his works. This was, as one college friend said to Tolkien, getting out of hand.

Most of what was going on just amused Tolkien. The idea of his becoming a cult, he found plain silly. At times he was annoyed by it all. There was the unannounced visitor who had come all the way from North America and simply had to have a photograph taken with the great man. And was that the pipe he had smoked when writing the book? No, now go away. Some of the books and essays written about him made Tolkien angry. People were trying to make his stories fit into their own lives and theories. That is not at all what my writing is for, he declared.

But we shouldn't see Tolkien as a stuffy Oxford Englishman who looked down on his success and pretended not to understand Americans. Tolkien was not such a person, and he was grateful for what his readers had done for him. He was neither a snob nor someone who was uncomfortable with foreigners. Except in one area. It wasn't that he disliked the French as such, it was just that he did not like French culture and thought that its influence on England was almost entirely negative. French food, French literature, French ideas — he pushed them as far away as he could. For

French wine, however, he would make an exception. And also for the French editions of *The Lord of the Rings*. Although, as was said to him at the time, the idea of Bilbo speaking French was about as ridiculous as that of Tolkien eating frogs' legs.

At this stage, however, Tolkien could have eaten and done pretty much whatever he wanted. The bills that had been a constant worry were now paid and the long years of struggling to be recognized were mostly over. He and Edith were living comfortably, their children were grown, and publishers and newspapers were eager to have this Oxford professor write for them. The two of them were determined not to allow fame to change their lives too drastically. They were too happy for that.

CHAPTER SIX

Just Another Teacher

NE of the most appealing aspects of Tolkien's character was his honesty. When he described himself as just another teacher doing what he did at Oxford, he actually meant it. He kept up his interest in the university rowing races, or boat races as they are known, for example, and always found it difficult to choose which one of the various colleges to support. He enjoyed watching rugby and encouraged his more athletic students to work as hard on the sports field as they did at their books. He sat on various college and university committees over the years, and served as sub-warden of Merton College. This job involved making public relations visits to some of the properties and land owned by the college, usually in some of the nicer parts of Leicestershire and Lincolnshire, in the middle of England. He always got along well with the farmers he met in these counties and is still remembered fondly, even by the children of some of the people he met all those years ago. They say that their parents spoke of the Oxford professor who became famous for his books, who was always so friendly, and who seemed to know so much about the land and about farming. He seemed, said their parents, to be one of us.

Tolkien was also a member of the Merton College Wine Committee, and this allowed him to sample and learn more about the wines he had come to love. There was one occasion when he went on holiday with the key to the wine cellars, meaning that the thirsty and quite demanding professors were without their wine while he was away. It took some time for him to live that down.

In 1967 the British author Humphrey Carpenter visited Tolkien in preparation for a biography that he was about to write on him. Carpenter found Tolkien to be a smaller man than he had expected. He writes, "Tallness is a quality of which he makes much in his books, so it is a little surprising to see that he himself is slightly less than average height — not much, but just enough to be noticeable. I introduce myself, and (since I made this appointment in advance and am expected) the quizzical and somewhat defensive look that first met me is replaced by a smile. A hand is offered and my own is firmly grasped.

"Behind him I can see the entrance-hall, which is small and tidy and contains nothing one would not expect in the house of a middle-class elderly couple. W.H. Auden [a highly respected and famous British poet], in an injudicious remark quoted in the newspapers, has called the house 'hideous', but that is nonsense. It is simply ordinary and suburban."

Carpenter meets Edith, a woman smaller than her husband and with tightly bound white hair and dark eyebrows. Then Tolkien and Carpenter go to the author's office, which is actually a garage at the side of the house. Tolkien tells his biographer that there is no car there because the couple have not owned one since the beginning of the Second World War. But there are lots and lots of books; piles of dictionaries of various languages; and an entire section devoted to *The Lord of the Rings*, with translations into Polish,

Danish, Dutch, Swedish, and Japanese. A map of Tolkien's Middle-earth is pinned to the wall.

Carpenter recalls that the study was rather cramped and that Tolkien apologized and explained that when another book was finished he and Edith might be able to move to a larger house. The room also had an electric fire, a blue alarm clock, and piles of letters from friends and readers. Carpenter writes that he could not always understand what Tolkien was saying, something that students sometimes said about his lectures. "He has a strange voice, deep but without resonance, entirely English but with some quality in it that I cannot define, as if he had come from another age of civilisation. Yet for much of the time he does not speak clearly. Words come out in eager rushes. Whole phrases are elided or compressed in the haste of emphasis. Often his hand comes up and grasps his mouth, which makes it even harder to hear him."

Carpenter also describes how Tolkien would suddenly put his pipe in his mouth and speak between clenched teeth and jaw, lighting a match at the end of a sentence as if to announce that he had stopped talking or to emphasize a point. He moved while he was talking, walking about the room and seeming to be bursting with energy and life. He would take a couple of puffs on his pipe and then knock it on an ashtray.

His hands were small and he wore a wedding ring. His clothes were rumpled but his figure was surprisingly good for a man of his age, with just a little plumpness around his stomach. He wore a colored vest, these being one of the few indulgences he had allowed himself since the success of his writing. The eyes were quick and sharp, moving from object to object and then focusing hard on something in particular. There were wrinkles around those eyes, which seemed to change shape and form as Tolkien concentrated. He was attentive, but not for very long periods. This, then, was Professor Tolkien.

Another person who met him was Desmond Albrow, who wrote about the encounter in the *Catholic Herald* in Britain. "He was the first Oxford professor that I had ever met face to face and the delightful fact was that he behaved to me like a true scholar-gentleman. I was then a fairly clever, but fairly callow, eighteen-year-old, fresh and unbruised by life from the North of England for whom Oxford at first taste was almost a foreign hinterland with bizarre rules and traps to snare both the arrogant and the innocent. In about a quarter of an hour Tolkien gave me a confidence and an optimism that he so easily could have destroyed with

Tolkien with pipe and book. A very usual pose.

a cutting phrase or a supercilious quip. Just imagine if I had encountered one of those modern-day, smart-alec, television-preening dons who have now despoiled what is left of the high tables of Oxford.

"Here was a professor who looked like a professor. Tolkien wore cords and a sports jacket, smoked a reassuring pipe, laughed a lot, sometimes mumbled when his thoughts outstripped words . . . There was a sense of civilisation, winsome sanity and sophistication about him."

A good man, a fair man, a kind man. Happy, too. There were difficult times, though, such as when his friend Jack Lewis died in 1963. The relationship between the two men had grown less close after Lewis's marriage, but they were still deeply fond of one another. Lewis's passing reminded Tolkien of his own mortality, but the letters from readers around the world reassured him of the immortality of his creations.

He also had his religious faith. The Roman Catholic Church underwent certain changes in the 1960s due to the Second Vatican Council, which was a huge gathering in Rome of Roman Catholic clergy to open the doors of the Church and introduce some reforms. In actual fact the reforms were minimal, but some members of the Church tried to exploit the council in order to disobey the Church and transform it, at least at a local level. Tolkien saw some of these sweeping changes happen to an institution he so dearly loved, and they didn't please him at all. But unlike some people who resisted any kind of change, Tolkien carried a faith that was deep and loving enough to accept reforms. They were annoying at times, he thought, but the truth of Catholicism was not altered because of them.

Tolkien retired from full-time teaching at Oxford in 1959, when he was sixty-seven and Edith seventy. He had taught for almost forty years and the time had certainly come. Edith was now becoming unwell, finding it increasingly difficult to walk due to her arthritis and suffering from poor digestion. The couple also simply wanted and needed more time together. Oxford was changing, and not for the better, according to Tolkien. He missed his older friends and the times of The Inklings and The Bird and Baby. Some of the new men weren't for him. He didn't understand them, and they didn't understand him. Tolkien was simply the product of a different generation, a different age, than these younger people.

He had taught all he had wanted to and had been recognized for his efforts. He had received honorary doctorates from Ireland and Belgium, literary awards, and requests to deliver prestigious lectures. On retirement he was asked to give his valedictory address, a farewell speech from a senior member, at Merton College Hall. Hundreds packed the hall. Several generations of professors and students were present, some brought there by their personal contact with Tolkien, others because they knew of him through his reputation at the university or because of his writing. Clouds of tobacco smoke rose above the heads of the crowd. Unlike today, people were allowed to smoke in such places in those days, and many were doing just that. As the audience waited for the guest of honor to appear, scores of small conversations were going on, a constant buzz filling this beautiful old building. Anticipation and excitement were high.

Then the official party comes to the stage, with Tolkien in the middle. They are wearing their university gowns and look splendid. A spontaneous thunder of clapping, and even cheers. Tolkien is introduced, and a few formalities are dealt with. Then Tolkien clears his throat and looks out at the audience, many of the faces familiar to him but others new and fresh. This is extended family, and the event marks a turning point in his life. He speaks of the glory that is Oxford, that is academic life, that is learning. There is emotion in his voice. He also makes some criticisms of the way the university is going and of the uniformity sweeping over higher education. We must allow, he says, students to explore and learn in their own way and not squeeze them into the shapes we want. To end his speech — and his time as a teacher at one of the finest universities in the world — he quotes from the "Namarie," an elvish song of farewell that he himself wrote. No better way to say goodbye. The audience understands. A silence. And then applause. Long and heartfelt applause. Tolkien sits down. It is time to go.

This, then, was his retirement, if it can be described as such. One of the ironies of Tolkien's life was that the older he grew, the more famous he became. He would receive telephone calls — mostly from the United States, often from California — early in the morning from people asking precise questions about Frodo or Gandalf. In an attempt to stop the constant disruption to the household, he went so far as to change his telephone number and take it out of the directory altogether. His address was kept a secret as well. Even so, he was forced to hire part-time secretaries to cope with all the correspondence.

He was known as an author to hundreds of thousands, but known as a person to far fewer. In fact, he and Edith sometimes felt quite isolated. Their children were now away and leading their own lives: Michael teaching in the Midlands, Christopher busy in Oxford with his own teaching work, Priscilla working as a probation officer on the other side of the city and also extremely busy, and John carrying out his duties as a priest with his own parish in Staffordshire. Tolkien's various secretaries often became family friends. As did academic colleagues such as the

Anglo-Saxon scholar Alistair Campbell and a former student, Norman Davis, who was the new Merton Professor of English Language and Literature.

In 1963 Tolkien was made an Honorary Fellow of Exeter College, and Merton made him an Emeritus Fellow. The latter title is one that is awarded to a retired teacher. These honors meant invitations to college dinners and functions, although he seldom went to them. Edith was not at all well and he was not going to leave her on her own for the sake of a dinner. In 1966 the couple celebrated their golden wedding anniversary and a great gathering was held at Merton College. Friends performed songs, and tributes and cards and telegrams came in from familiar and — to the couple's delight — unfamiliar quarters. People they had never met sent telegrams and letters; Sir Stanley Unwin sent fifty golden roses; others composed rhymes based on Tolkien's work to commemorate the event.

Tolkien continued to write, still working on *The Silmarillion*, which he was determined would one day be published. He worked on essays and poetry and was still devising new alphabets, and finished a story called *Smith of Wootton Major*. This tale had its origins in a request by an American publisher for Tolkien to write an introduction to George Macdonald's *The Golden Key*. Tolkien received such requests quite often and usually said no, but this was different. Macdonald, of course, had been a great influence on the young Tolkien and had remained an inspiration ever since. The foreword to *The Golden Key* took on a life of its own, and in turn became a separate work. There would be no introduction to Macdonald, but a new Tolkien story instead.

Tolkien enjoyed this urge to write a fresh story, something he had not felt in some time. He worked on it on a typewriter, which he had not done before. The story was partly autobiographical, in that the character of Smith, with his imagination and need to wonder, is clearly the now aged Tolkien looking back on his life. He showed it to Rayner Unwin, who initially thought it too short to stand on its own but eventually did publish it as a single book. The critics were generally positive, but the sales were nothing like those of *The Lord of the Rings* or *The Hobbit*. Tolkien also revised an earlier lecture called "On Fairy-Stories" and published it in 1964, along with a story called "Leaf by Niggle," in a book entitled *Tree and Leaf*. His eighty-nine-year-old aunt, Jane Neave, asked him for a book — a small book that old people could manage — about Tom Bombadil, a character from *The Lord of the Rings*. Tolkien obliged, and *The Adventures of Tom Bombadil* appeared accordingly, just months before his aunt died.

But Oxford was different now, and so was life. Edith was increasingly ill and walking was becoming too painful for her. Trips to the seaside were virtually impossible and the house in Headington, which was now a suburb of Oxford, just wasn't suited to them anymore. Without the children, it was too big — they rattled in it. They were financially secure, so they thought of moving to a new home, one that would give them more pleasure. But where? They had been spending holidays in Bournemouth for some time and both of them enjoyed it very much. This town on England's south coast offered a warmer climate, which was better for Edith's arthritis. And Tolkien loved the sea and the walks along the promenade. Bournemouth it would be.

Although this town can hardly be called fashionable, that does nothing to diminish its appeal. In some ways it increases it. Close by are forest walks, with huge pine trees forming secret enclosures of green and cone. Throughout the years, Edith had stayed at the Hotel Miramar with the children, often when her husband was away lecturing; more recently Tolkien had started to accompany her. Edith enjoyed the company at the hotel and in Bournemouth, Tolkien less so. But he could work away in his hotel room with its magnificent view. There was also a good Roman Catholic church nearby and plenty of taxis to take them wherever they wanted to go.

In August 1968 they made the move to 19 Lakeside Road, a bungalow they had seen only once earlier, the day before they purchased it. For the first time in their lives Tolkien and Edith had central heating and a bathroom each. Once again the garage became Tolkien's study, and again a part-time secretary had to be employed. The couple had a fine new kitchen with modern appliances, and they could sit on their large verandah in the evenings. There was a good garden, and at the bottom of it a little gate that led to a small wood known as Branksome Chine. (Strangely enough, I used to walk there with my mother and aunt when I was a

Bournemouth, where the Tolkiens lived in their later years, and where Edith died.

child. I was told that Robin Hood was hiding in the trees with his merry men. My mother and my Auntie Ethel were wrong, of course. It wasn't Robin, it was Frodo.)

After the wood came the sea. The cry of the gulls, the feel of the sand, and the gentle whistle of the salty wind. This would do nicely. And Catholic neighbors lived nearby, who would take Tolkien to church. Edith also attended, though rarely. The couple also had some domestic help, giving them the kind of luxury they had never before known.

Of course there was work to be done if Tolkien wished to do it. *The Silmarillion* still wasn't finished, and newspapers and magazines were always willing to take book reviews and articles he might care to write. Mail continued to arrive from readers, with requests to name animals, cars, and even children after characters from *The Lord of the Rings*. Of course you can, he usually replied, and I'll even give you some more names for the future. But a game of solitaire or a good read were often so much more satisfying. And there was Edith. She had a fine doctor, but her health was still deteriorating. He had to spend time with her. Just in case.

It was the middle of November, a Friday night. Edith had an inflamed gallbladder, painful and distressing. Many of the symptoms of this problem resemble those of a heart attack, and while advanced and relatively straightforward surgery to deal with the problem exists today, things weren't quite so simple in 1971. Edith was eighty-two and no medical complaint is straightforward at that age. She was soon at the hospital. She fought hard, but her health was not good and she was weak. Tolkien prays, as do friends and family. Just a few more years with Edith, O God, just a little longer. More days of pain and suffering, and then, when the end comes, a release. It is Monday, November 29. Edith is dead. Tolkien writes to a friend, explaining how courageous she had been and that he "cannot lift up his heart," his pain is so great.

He can say and do nothing for some days. Eventually he is able to speak and write to his loved ones, to his children. He tells his children he has decided that the inscription on the gravestone should be simple: "Edith Mary Tolkien, 1889–1971. Lúthien." Lúthien? Where did this name come from, when he had always referred to Edith as "mummy" to his sons and daughter? Lúthien was a character in his still uncompleted work *The Silmarillion*. She was the most beautiful maiden ever to walk in Middle-earth, and was based on his own Edith, the pure and innocent girl who had danced for him so many years ago and who had inspired everything — books, children, love. Lúthien.

He tells his children — and we can only imagine the tears welling up in his eyes — that Edith was, and had always known she was, his Lúthien. Goodnight Edith. Goodnight Lúthien.

It had been a good marriage. Yet some critics have tried to find sorrow and failure in it. They search in vain. He was a good husband and she was a good wife. There were times when they argued, but this is inevitable as well as necessary. A true combining of souls does not mean an evaporation of the individual will. Edith was not always as devoted a Catholic as Tolkien, but their disagreements probably brought them closer together. They shared a pure love for their children and grandchildren, and always put them first. They had both been orphaned at an early age and from the first had connected with one another, completed one another.

Joseph Pearce, in his remarkable book on Tolkien entitled *Tolkien: Man and Myth*, reminds us that "friends of the Tolkiens remembered the deep affection between them, which was visible in the care with which they chose and wrapped each other's birthday presents and the great concern they showed for each other's health." Some say that Tolkien's great legacy is *The Hobbit* and *The Lord of the Rings* and that his marriage and family are not important. But without marriage and family there would have been no Bilbo, Frodo, Gandalf, hobbits, and books! Like one of the trees he so loved, Tolkien would have blown down with any passing wind and his genius would have been crushed, without the love he had for Edith and the adoration she lavished on him.

So great the love, so great the pain. Yes, he still had the children and good friends, but nothing could replace his wife. What would he do and where would he go next?

CHAPTER SEVEN

End Times

OLKIEN couldn't stay in Bournemouth anymore. There were too many reminders of Edith's pain and passing, and anyway the sense of isolation was too great and the arrangements simply weren't practical. Oxford was the only alternative, but it wasn't clear where he was going to live. Merton College came to the rescue, offering Tolkien a set of rooms in a college house on Merton Street, where a domestic worker and his wife could look after him. These domestic workers at Oxford were called scouts, and they sometimes became friends with the students and professors they served. Indeed, the relationship could be more like that of a family than that of employee and employer.

Meals would be cooked for Tolkien, his clothes washed, his rooms tidied, and even the bed made if he so desired it. Retired teachers were not usually provided for in this way, and it is a tribute not so much to Tolkien's fame but to how much he was liked at Oxford that such an offer was made. Of course he accepted, the thought of such an arrangement raising his spirits for the first time since Edith's death. He was back in Oxford by early March of 1972. And how typical of Tolkien that he struck up a friendship with the men who came to move his belongings from Bournemouth to

Oxford and rode with them in their truck for the whole journey.

The apartment on Merton Street couldn't have been better. He had use of a bedroom and bathroom, plus a large sitting room; and the scout, Charlie Carr, and his wife, Mavis, lived in the basement. Tolkien was not always well in these years and the Carrs were always on hand to help out and even provide some company. He became friendly with the couple and particularly enjoyed playing with their two young granddaughters when they visited.

If he became tired of his rooms he could meet with old friends, and some new young ones, somewhere else in Oxford. There was the Eastgate Hotel right next door, where he had drunk and dined with Jack Lewis and some of the Inklings. And he was always welcome in the college itself, where the meals were free and the company guaranteed. Although Tolkien, now wealthy, was always generous to other people, he saw no reason in squandering money on himself if it was not necessary.

And his tastes remained the same. English food was always his preference, good and plain English food. Bacon and eggs for breakfast; some toast, too; and a pot of strong tea. Roast beef and plenty of potatoes later in the day, for lunch or dinner. For dessert he liked a trifle or, in summer, strawberries with lots of cream. More tea was welcome — it was welcome throughout the day, in fact. And along with tea he enjoyed fruit cake, homemade if possible, though some of the cakes now sold in the local stores, even in the chain stores, he quite liked. He might also have a bar of milk chocolate in the afternoon if he felt like it, and cocoa was good just before bed. Always the pipe, of course, from breakfast right on until lights out.

With this new lifestyle came a certain degree of loneliness, but also a certain degree of independence. Tolkien was always a surprisingly fit man, considering his constant smoking and lack of exercise aside

21 Merton Street in Oxford, where Tolkien went to live after his wife Edith's death.

from walking and some cycling when he was younger. He was a frequent visitor to his son Christopher's home in a village just outside of Oxford, and would delight in playing with grandchildren Rachel and Adam. There was a holiday in Sidmouth with Priscilla and some trips to see his brother, Hilary, who was still living in Evesham and working on his farm.

He watched some television, which he had not started to do until fairly recently. He particularly liked watching sports; cricket and tennis were his favorites, but he also enjoyed the coverage of rugby when it was on. Not enough of it, he complained. As for most of the light entertainment and news, he was less interested. In the past he'd never been a follower of the news, and it was too late to start now. He liked a glass of good whisky as well. Single malt was the only type to drink, a taste that he had discovered long ago and that was reinforced by the ready availability of some of the best scotches in Oxford's senior common rooms, where teachers and professors gathered to relax.

Douglas Gilbert was a photographer who met Tolkien at this time and liked him very much indeed. "When I went to see him he was playfully using his walking stick as a fencing sword with me, and there is one photo where his stick is partially raised, hinting at this, and the expression on his face is one of glee. Like a child in a way, so happy. I had been in England all summer of 1972 and had gotten no reply from Tolkien to many letters and phone calls. When I returned in January the following year, Mr. Colin Hardie, a friend of Tolkien's, said that he would help me. 'I'm not afraid of Ronnie,' he said. Because Tolkien was known to have refused many people and had a reputation for being quite fierce if he wanted to be. Colin set up the interview and walked me to Tolkien's rooms and introduced me. Tolkien was totally charming and accommodating and gave no hint of displeasure with any of it. What a remarkable man."

A remarkable man indeed, but also an old one. He celebrated his eightieth birthday in 1972 and there were signs that his health was taking something of a beating. He seemed to know this because he finally admitted that he would never complete and edit *The Silmarillion* and effectively passed the project on to his son Christopher. He received the Commander of the Order of the British Empire from the queen at Buckingham Palace in 1972, and in the same year he received an Honorary Doctorate of Letters from the University of Oxford. Both were great honors. The following summer he went up to Edinburgh, Scotland, with Priscilla to receive his latest public award. But when he returned from Scotland he was not feeling very well. He had been suffering from indigestion for some time and far from getting better, as the doctor had said he would, he was getting much worse.

He had an X-ray at the hospital but it revealed nothing. He was put on a special diet, which annoyed him more than he could say. He was also told that he could no longer drink wine, but to tell the truth, it no longer pleased him very much and he could barely taste it. Friends thought the worst was coming now. His time had come, one of them said, and it was now just a matter of the great man unwinding and calling it a day.

Yet he still felt well enough to make a trip back to Bournemouth to visit Denis and Jocelyn Tolhurst, the doctor and his wife who had looked after him and Edith when they had lived in the town. There was a birthday party for a mutual friend and Tolkien drank some champagne. But during the night he felt unwell and began to complain of increasing pain. The next morning he was taken to a private hospital, where the doctors diagnosed a bleeding gastric ulcer. There was no family around right at that time because Michael was on holiday in Switzerland and Christopher was in

France. John and Priscilla rushed down to the south coast to be with their father. They arrived the following day and were told by the hospital staff that he might recover.

It was not to be. An infection had developed in his chest. And on the Sunday morning of September 2, 1973, only a few days after he had been admitted, with the sea breeze flapping at the curtains in his room and the welcoming calls of the gulls surrounding the hospital, John Ronald Reuel Tolkien, creator of *The Hobbit* and *The Lord of the Rings* and one of the most beloved authors in the history of language, crossed over to a paradise he had always known existed. Tolkien was dead at eighty-one years old.

His requiem mass was held in Oxford four days later at the Church of St. Anthony of Padua, the Headington church in which he had worshipped and prayed so often. His son John chose the readings and celebrated the mass, assisted by Father Robert Murray, who was an old friend of Tolkien's, along with the parish priest Monsignor Doran. The church was full, and full of love and tears. Tolkien was buried in the Catholic cemetery at Wolvercote, just outside of Oxford, alongside his wife and best friend, Edith. He had composed the inscription on their joint gravestone, remembering her as Lúthien. Now added to this were his name and dates and then "Beren," the name of Lúthien's lover in *The Silmarillion*. A love of mythological proportions was given flesh and blood in Tolkien and his wife, Edith.

The *Daily Telegraph* obituary read as follows: "Bilbo found a scrap of black twist and tied it round his arm. The little hobbit wept bitterly. Somewhere in the world of fantasy that Prof. J.R.R. Tolkien created, this is happening at the news of his death. His creatures were so real, elf princes, hobbits, ents, trolls, orcs and other grim enemies, that the Merton Professor of the English language has acquired, like them, a certain timelessness. He was Gandalf the ageless Wizard, appearing and shaping the destiny of vast upland kingdoms, full of imagery and the twilight of pre-history. Even at the ripe age of 81, it is sad to lose one who brought so much fresh air and poetry into our literature. The kingdoms that he created will not pass away."

Indeed not. We have not lost him, nor he us. Those who really knew him and understood him saw that at his funeral. Because as the small group of people who had been invited to the gravesite were leaving, some of them, just some, said they heard a sound in the bushes in front of the trees. There was nothing there, at least to most eyes. "Be quiet," says Frodo, "you almost gave us away. Be quiet!" And behind him is a line of humans and other creatures, stretching for mile after mile. The creatures are Tolkien's creations, of course. The humans? There are millions of them. They are the happy, smiling faces of his readers — past, present, and yes, yet to come. The story never ends. He always knew that.

Bibliography

BOOKS BY J.R.R. TOLKIEN

These are some of the works by J.R.R. Tolkien that were published during his lifetime. I have included the names of the original publishers, but the works are now available in many and various editions.

Sir Gawain and the Green Knight. Edited by J.R.R. Tolkien and E.V. Gordon. Oxford: Clarendon Press, 1925.

The Hobbit: or There and Back Again. London: George Allen and Unwin, 1937.

"On Fairy-Stories." In Essays Presented to Charles Williams. London: Oxford University Press, 1947.

Farmer Giles of Ham. London: George Allen and Unwin, 1949.

The Fellowship of the Ring: Being the first part of The Lord of the Rings. London: George Allen and Unwin, 1954.

The Two Towers: Being the second part of The Lord of the Rings. London: George Allen and Unwin, 1954.

The Return of the King: Being the third part of The Lord of the Rings. London: George Allen and Unwin, 1955.

The Adventures of Tom Bombadil and Other Verses from the Red Book. London: George Allen and Unwin, 1962.

Tree and Leaf. London: George Allen and Unwin, 1964.

Smith of Wootton Major. London: George Allen and Unwin, 1967.

As well as these titles, others by Tolkien were published after his death. They include uncompleted works that were later edited and collections of essays. Tolkien's son Christopher has also edited twelve volumes of the History of Middle-earth series.

The Father Christmas Letters. Edited by Baillie Tolkien. London: George Allen and Unwin, 1976.

The Silmarillion. Edited by Christopher Tolkien. London: George Allen and Unwin, 1977.

Unfinished Tales of Númenor and Middle-earth. Edited by Christopher Tolkien. London: George Allen and Unwin, 1980.

The Letters of J.R.R. Tolkien. Edited by Humphrey Carpenter with Christopher Tolkien. London: George Allen and Unwin, 1981.

Mr. Bliss. London: George Allen and Unwin, 1982.

Finn and Hengest: The Fragment and the Episode. Edited by Alan Bliss. London: George Allen and Unwin, 1982.

The Monsters and the Critics and Other Essays. Edited by Christopher Tolkien. London: George Allen and Unwin, 1983.

BOOKS ABOUT J.R.R. TOLKIEN

There are several books about Tolkien but some of them, frankly, are to be avoided. The following are very good indeed.

Carpenter, Humphrey. *J.R.R. Tolkien: A Biography*. London: George Allen and Unwin, 1977.

Carpenter, Humphrey. *The Inklings: C.S. Lewis, J.R.R. Tolkien, Charles Williams, and their friends*. London: George Allen and Unwin, 1978.

Foster, Robert. *The Complete Guide to Middle-earth: from* The Hobbit *to* The Silmarillion. New York: Ballantine Books, 1978.

Pearce, Joseph. *Tolkien: Man and Myth*. San Francisco: Ignatius, 1998.

Rosebury, Brian. *Tolkien: A Critical Assessment*. New York: St. Martin's Press, 1992.

Tolkien, John, and Priscilla Tolkien. *The Tolkien Family Album*. New York: Houghton Mifflin, 1992.

Acknowledgements

The problem with thanking people is, try as you might, you always manage to forget someone. To those whom I have so foolishly treated, I am sorry. My warmest thanks to Nelson Doucet, Don Bastian, Siobhan Blessing, and everybody else at Stoddart Publishing. What a publisher should be. My thanks also to Humphrey Carpenter, Joseph Pearce, Douglas Gilbert, the Birmingham Oratory, my wife Bernadette and our children Daniel, Lucy, Oliver, and Elizabeth.

About the Author

Michael Coren is also the author of biographies of G.K. Chesterton, H.G. Wells, C.S. Lewis and Sir Arthur Conan Doyle. He is a radio and television broadcaster and syndicated columnist based in Toronto.

Index

Picture Sources

p. 3, © Douglas Gilbert

p. 15, © Jonathan Berg/Birmingham Picture Library

p. 17, 19 and 21, courtesy of Birmingham Oratory

p. 23, © Thomas Photos, Oxford, England

pp. 28–29, © Thomas Photos

p. 36, Canadian Press

p. 40, Leeds University Archives

pp. 42–43, © Thomas Photos

p. 51 and 53, © Thomas Photos

p. 55, © Ian Britton

p. 57, used by permission of The Marion E. Wade Center, Wheaton College,
    Illinois/Wolf Suschitzky

pp. 60–61, © Douglas Gilbert

p. 63, used by permission of The Marion E. Wade Center/Stephen
    W. Mead

p. 72, © George Allen & Unwin Ltd., 1966, and © HarperCollins
    Publishers, 1999

p. 76, © HarperCollins Publishers, 1999

p. 79, © Hulton Getty

p. 82, © Thomas Photos

p. 89, © HarperCollins Publishers, 1993, and © Ballantine Books

p. 97 and 105, © Douglas Gilbert

p. 107, © Hulton Getty

p. 113, © Ian Britton

p. 121 and 125, courtesy of Patrick Blessing